THE GLORIOUS YEARS OF THE GNR

GREAT NORTHERN RAILWAY

JOHN RYAN

GREAT NORTHERN

ACKNOWLEDGEMENTS

I would like to express my gratitude to David P Williams for his considerable help in producing colour versions of monochrome images taken before the days of colour photography, in this volume and also the earlier book *The Glorious Days of the LNER*.

I would like to thank the following people for their help. Roger Arnold, David Burrill, John Chalcraft, Peter Crangle, John Law, Hugh Parkin.

Unless otherwise stated, all photographs from the author's collection.

Great Northern Books Limited
PO Box 1380, Bradford, BD5 5FB
www.greatnorthernbooks.co.uk

© John Ryan 2023

Every effort has been made to acknowledge correctly and contact the copyright holders of material in this book. Great Northern Books Ltd apologises for any unintentional errors or omissions, which should be notified to the publisher.

All rights reserved. No part of this book may be reproduced in any form or by any means without permission in writing from the publisher, except by a reviewer who may quote brief passages in a review.

ISBN: 978-1-914227-45-5

Design and layout: David Burrill

CIP Data
A catalogue for this book is available from the British Library

INTRODUCTION

In 2023, one hundred years have passed from the dissolution of the Great Northern Railway. Formed in the mid-1840s, the company was instrumental in connecting London with the eastern half of England, the North East and Scotland. Later, the GNR made inroads into other parts of the country, such as Nottinghamshire and West Yorkshire. From this base, the GNR successfully served the population for a number of years and was able to innovate in several areas, with developments in locomotive design, carriage construction and services offered. In an era before the motor car, when the world was horse-drawn and steam-powered, the GNR was part of a 'golden age' of British history.

By the mid-1840s, travel between London and the North East was possible via a circuitous route through the Midlands before cutting across the country to York. A direct line from London to York had been surveyed as early as 1835, yet serious thought to the undertaking was not given until the 'railway mania' of the 1840s. Two schemes were in motion at this time, the London & York and the Cambridge & York, with both soon realising their interests would be served advantageously by pooling resources and a Joint Committee was formed on 17th May 1844.

William Cubitt was engaged as engineer for the project and planned the main line from London to York, with a loop from Peterborough to Lincoln and Boston, as well as branches to Sheffield and Wakefield. The estimated cost of the over 300 miles of railway was £6,500,000. Submitted to Parliament in 1845, the bill met opposition from parties influenced by George Hudson, whose interests in the Midland route to York clashed with the London & York. Ultimately, the bill was passed in mid-1846, minus the Sheffield and Wakefield branches.

The section from Peterborough to Boston and Lincoln was deemed the easiest to construct and this work was put in hand first during early 1847. Despite a downturn in the financial market, the line was ready for traffic on 17th October 1848. Several contractors were engaged for the London to Peterborough line and progress was steady to completion in mid-1850. A special train ran for the Great Northern Railway officials on 5th August, whilst the public was carried from the 7th August. Peterborough was reached in two hours 30 minutes. From the 8th, services to York were offered, with trains running via the loop and the York & North Midland Railway to York, whilst the first train to Edinburgh departed on 2nd September. Nearly two years had to pass for the route from Peterborough to Retford through Grantham to be ready and conclude the original project, not forgetting the completion of King's Cross station.

Whilst the construction of the main line was progressing, the GNR entered into agreements with other railway companies to gain access to lucrative areas. The Manchester, Sheffield & Lincolnshire Railway allowed a connection at Retford for the GNR to run to Sheffield. At Grantham, the Ambergate, Nottingham, Boston & Eastern Junction Railway joined the two routes. Yet, several disputes with the Midland Railway at Nottingham seriously affected operations, leading to an independent station being built and the GNR formally absorbed the ANB&EJR in 1861. Further north, the Lancashire & Yorkshire provided a section of rails necessary to take the GNR to Leeds. Several local lines connected to the city, delivering the necessary springboards to Halifax, Bradford and Wakefield. Within the next decade or so, the company had absorbed many of these routes to secure a strong position in West Yorkshire.

In Nottinghamshire, the Midland Railway dominated traffic and exploited local businesses beyond reasonable limits. The GNR was encouraged to provide competition, particularly for coal traffic which resulted in the Derbyshire & Staffordshire extension of the 1870s. From the original route to the city, the GNR forged northward through the Erewash Valley towards Alfreton and Pinxton. Westward, the line reached Derby and Burton upon Trent (the latter via the North Staffordshire Railway). The Stafford & Uttoxeter Railway was purchased in the early 1880s and this connected with the London & North Western Railway. The approximate cost for the Derbyshire & Staffordshire extension was £2,500,000.

Although the GNR spearheaded this project, two others were undertaken with the help of other main line railway companies. In the late 1850s, the relationship with the Manchester, Sheffield & Lincolnshire Railway was expanded to compete with the LNWR around Manchester, Liverpool and Cheshire. Known as the Cheshire Lines Committee, which later saw the Midland Railway added as a partner, the company offered an alternative route between Manchester and Liverpool via Warrington. The line northward reached Southport while that southward ended at Chester, going via Altrincham and Northwich. Overcoming the animosity with the MR in Nottingham, the GNR expanded into East Anglia with the company to form the Midland & Great Northern Railway in the late 1880s/early 1890s. The pair bought several amalgamated railways in the area which had encountered financial difficulties. The Great Eastern Railway dominated Eastern England and the GNR also had a joint line with the company which ran from March to Doncaster and opened in the early 1880s.

A long-term project for the GNR was the development of lines in Lincolnshire. Reaching many of the important places in the county with the loop, the East Lincolnshire Railway from Boston to Grimsby was leased in the late 1840s further expanding the area served. Before Grouping, several connections had been made, including

Boston-Sleaford-Barkston, the Horncastle branch, the Kirkstead-Little Steeping cut-off, and the development of seaside resorts at Mablethorpe, Skegness and Sutton-on-Sea.

To serve the company's locomotive needs initially, Benjamin Cubitt (William's brother) ordered a large number of locomotives from contractors to their proprietary designs. In 1850, Archibald Sturrock became the GNR's first long-term Locomotive Engineer, holding the position for 15 years until taking early retirement. Under financial restraints, he was able to develop the foundation for future GNR locomotives by designing well-boilered, robust engines for the East Coast passenger traffic. He also made a bold attempt to increase the haulage capacity of goods 0-6-0s by providing a steam engine for the tender wheels.

Patrick Stirling was initially appointed as Doncaster Works Manager in early 1866 before quickly moving up to Locomotive Engineer. He was able to enjoy the use of Doncaster Works, which soon after he took the job built the first locomotive on site, whereas only repairs had been carried out previously. With new construction, Stirling was able to replace older engines. In turn, this improved maintenance due to better techniques and practices as the steam locomotive developed. Stirling's most important design was the 8 ft 'Single' and this dominated GNR main line passenger traffic for much of the late 1800s. As a result, the locomotives and their designer became world-famous.

This, and his advancing age, contributed to Stirling's unwillingness to modernise his engineering philosophy. His successor in 1896 was H.A. Ivatt and he faced the problem of growing traffic requirements. Ivatt addressed these by introducing the 4-4-2 'Atlantic'-type to Britain and a numerous class of these – with large diameter boilers – was built for the main line traffic.

H.N. Gresley (later knighted) started at Doncaster in the Carriage and Wagon Department in 1905 and was promoted when Ivatt retired in 1911. At this time, the GNR locomotive stock had a firm base and Gresley was left to experiment with several ideas. He started with feedwater heaters before moving on to three cylinders and his own design of valve gear, where the outside sets operated that for the centre cylinder. This became a feature of all his subsequent locomotives. Gresley was also the first in Britain to fully adopt the 4-6-2 'Pacific' wheel arrangement and this type became a mainstay on the East Coast Main Line to dieselisation in the early 1960s. Arguably, Gresley's time on the GNR was instrumental in his later success as Chief Mechanical Engineer of the London & North Eastern Railway, 1923-1941.

The GNR began carriage construction at Doncaster around ten years before locomotives. Several innovations were boasted by the company subsequently, including: restaurant carriage; side-corridor coach; articulation; electric cooking equipment. In addition to the GNR's own carriages, Doncaster Works built vehicles for the East Coast Joint Stock which saw the company join with the North Eastern and North British Railways to provide a pool of coaches that ran through on the East Coast Main Line. As the GNR had the longest section, the company took a leading role in the venture.

As mentioned, Doncaster Works was founded in the early 1850s, beating competition from Boston and Peterborough. In around 15 years, both locomotives and carriages were being constructed on site and as time progressed wagons were built in addition to many components used for the rolling stock. Initially occupying 28 acres on the western side of the station, the site expanded considerably as the company grew. In the late 19th century, the Wagon Works moved just to the south, whilst an impressive repair works, the Crimpsall, was constructed on land connected to the original site, being operational from the early 1900s. At this period, the workforce numbered around 3,000-4,000. During the First World War, roles vacated by men left for the Armed Forces were filled by women. They were also instrumental in the production of shells and other war materials at the works.

The GNR developed at the same time as photographic technology. Many of the new early railways were illustrated by traditional methods, yet these were soon overtaken by photographs, with railway manufacturers being at the forefront to illustrate their new creations. At Doncaster, the GNR contracted a local firm, usually Bagshaw & Son around the turn of the century, before setting up a Photography Department in 1905. A whole-plate field camera was used from this date until the early 1950s when a replacement was sought following damage caused to the original after being blown over by a strong gust of wind. Locomotives, carriages, wagons, personnel and new additions to the site at Doncaster were all captured. Elsewhere, both professional and amateur photographers were eager to record the new railways, giving rise to a key feature of being a railway enthusiast – making images of locomotives at work.

Being a proud Doncastrian, with connections to Doncaster 'Plant' Works, the GNR has always held an interest for me and hopefully the company's proud history has been well-illustrated in this collection.

John Ryan
Over Peover, January 2023

EARLY LOCOMOTIVES AND REBUILDS

Above ARCHIBALD STURROCK
After the formation of the Great Northern Railway in the mid-1840s, the company's Civil Engineer, William Cubitt, suggested to the Board that his brother, Benjamin, would be a good candidate for the position of Locomotive Engineer. This proposal was subsequently accepted and Benjamin was appointed in November 1846. Sadly, he served the GNR for just over 12 months as his death occurred on 12th January 1848 at age 53. Nevertheless, during his tenure he worked diligently to provide the company with motive power to meet operational requirements. Around 100 locomotives were ordered from contractors to their own designs, as this was the practice of the time. Benjamin Cubitt was succeeded by Edward Bury, who mainly developed coaching stock for the company and also formulated plans for the workshops at Doncaster before leaving the GNR in early 1850. From over 40 applicants for the vacant position, Archibald Sturrock was chosen to head the Locomotive and Rolling Stock departments, as well as the new facilities at Doncaster for construction and repair. He left the Great Western Railway where he had been a pupil of Daniel Gooch and Isambard Kingdom Brunel. Sturrock was influenced by the latter pair's work and adapted their use of high heating surfaces and boiler pressures for standard gauge locomotives. During his tenure, Sturrock was somewhat restricted by financial considerations and often had to rebuild older locomotives to meet requirements. An innovation which came about as a result was the use of a tender with a steam engine providing auxiliary power. Sturrock was the beneficiary of a legacy in the mid-1860s and he retired soon after, being succeeded by Patrick Stirling.

Above **400 CLASS 0-6-0 NO. 400**
The reconstruction of a few older locomotives proved the worthiness of Sturrock's steam tender plans and induced the GNR Board to authorise new construction. This was done in February 1864 and initially comprised 20 locomotives, with ten each from Kitson & Co. and R.W. Hawthorn & Co. The order appeared during early 1865, with no. 400 deemed the first and built by the aforementioned in January. The locomotive is seen here at Doncaster Works before numbering at the time – note the connecting rods on the tender wheels and chimney at the rear of the coal space. No. 400 was in service to late 1899. The steam tender was abandoned early on, and no. 400's was rebuilt in the late 1860s.

Below **SHARP 2-2-2 'SINGLE' NO. 45**
Early passenger locomotives were ordered from Sharp Brothers & Co., Manchester, to their proprietary 2-2-2 'single' design. Numbering six initially, the builder offered the GNR favourable terms to enlarge the order. These were accepted, adding another 44 'singles' for construction to the end of the 1840s. No. 45, pictured, was amongst the final engines dispatched to the GNR and taken into stock during early 1850.

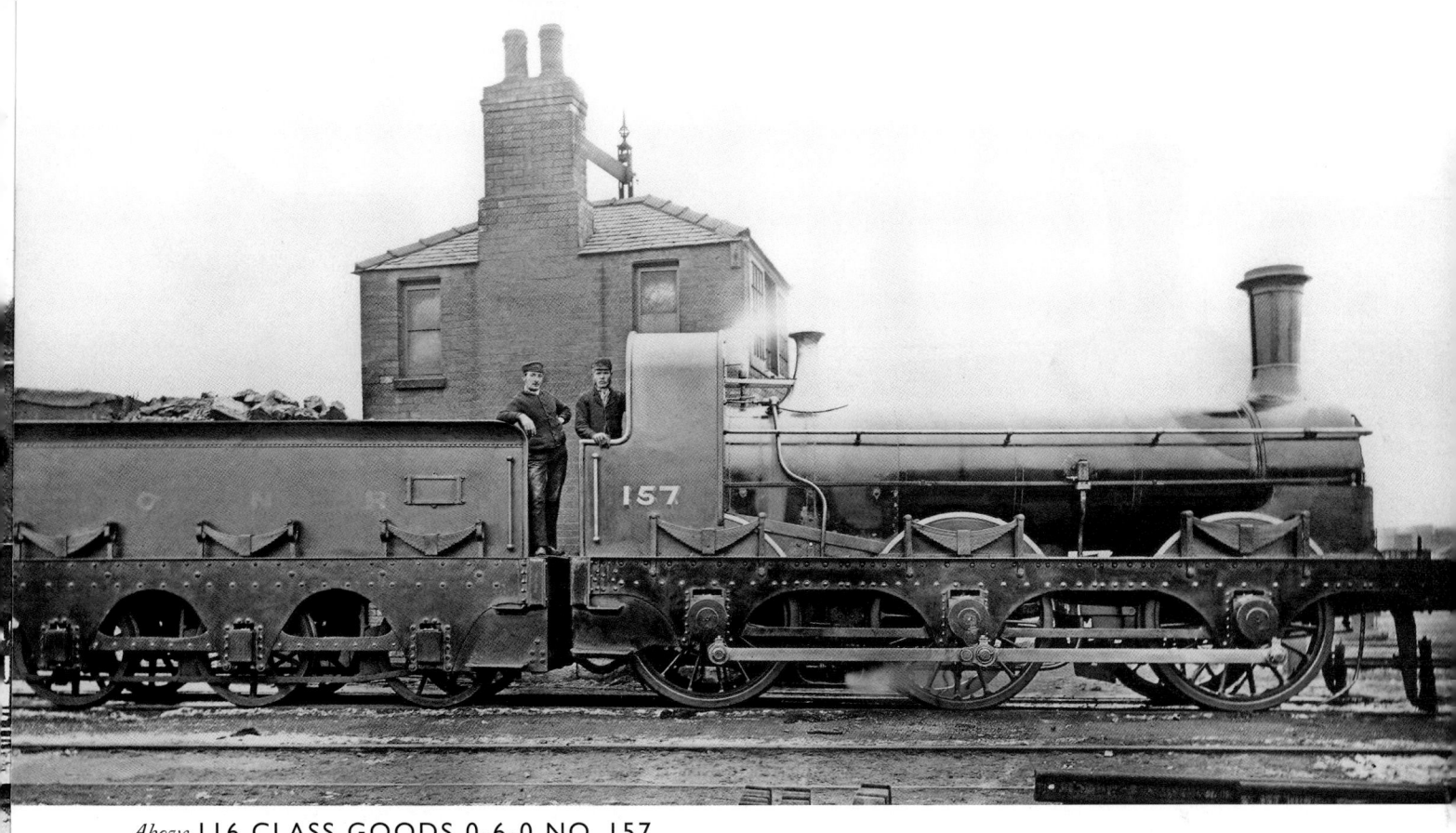

Above **116 CLASS GOODS 0-6-0 NO. 157**
Early in 1850, 30 0-6-0 goods locomotives were ordered, with half from E.B. Wilson and R.W. Hawthorn & Co. No. 157 was amongst those completed by the first mentioned. All comprised GNR Class 116 and partially designed by Sturrock. Later, some were reboilered by Stirling and no. 157 has been treated here.

Below **308 CLASS GOODS 0-6-0 NO. 319**
Nasmyth & Co.-built Sturrock 308 Class no. 319 has the crew happily posing in this image.

Above **STURROCK 0-8-0T NO. 472**
Another concern with the opening of the Metropolitan Railway's City lines was the transport of freight to various connecting yards. This required a specialised locomotive which was both powerful and capable of working within the restrictions of the line. Sturrock became aware of an 0-8-0T locomotive built by the Avonside Engine Co. which was suggested to be suitable and after viewing the type in service he ordered two of a similar design. These were in traffic by mid-1866 and only found limited use on the route as the engines disrupted the permanent way and were left to work in King's Cross goods yard. As a result, the lifespan of the 0-8-0Ts was limited and both, nos 472 and 473, were condemned during 1880. No. 472 is at King's Cross here.

Opposite above **STURROCK 241 CLASS 0-4-2T NO. 243A**
Another view of no. 243A, but in comparison to the previous image several changes have taken place. The main one being a new, slightly smaller, domeless boiler has been fitted, whilst coal rails have been provided to the coal space. Another concerns the maker's plate which was affixed to the tank/coal space side and encircled by a Great Northern Railway plate. This has been removed to show the company's initials only and the number has been painted on the cab side. The transformation took place c. 1880 and the engine was in service until the turn of the century.

Opposite below **STURROCK 270 CLASS 0-4-2T NO. 277**
With ten 241 Class 0-4-2T locomotives in service for the London suburban traffic, Sturrock envisaged more engines for work as services expanded, particularly to areas outlying the capital. Initially wanting 15 locomotives, Sturrock was only authorised to obtain ten and these entered traffic during early 1867. Their sphere of operation was wider and the height restrictions on the 241 Class were obviated, resulting in some changes. A reclassification as the 270 Class occurred as a result. Again, the order was split between two manufacturers: Neilson & Co. and Avonside Engine Co. The latter was responsible for the erection of no. 277 which has a local service here. Reconstruction with a Stirling boiler has occurred placing the image post-1880 and before withdrawal in 1900. Whilst all the 241 Class moved on to the duplicate list, only four of the 270 Class did, with no. 277 one of six remaining off the list.

STURROCK 251 CLASS 2-4-0 NO. 256

One of the last classes to enter service under Sturrock was the 251 2-4-0. Ten were built by Sharp, Stewart & Co, with no. 256 amidst this number and in traffic from April 1866. The engine was subsequently equipped with a Stirling boiler and has the modification in this image as crew pose for the camera.

Above **STURROCK 270 CLASS 0-4-2T NO. 279**
A pause in shunting duties at an unidentified location has occurred, allowing this picture of Sturrock 270 Class 0-4-2T no. 279 to be taken in the 1880s/1890s. The locomotive was the last of the class to be constructed by the Avonside Engine Co. in April 1867. In October 1880, a Stirling 4 ft 5 in. diameter boiler was fitted and is present here. No. 279 was placed on the duplicate list during May 1904 and worked for another year before withdrawn from traffic.

Below **STURROCK 251 CLASS 2-4-0 NO. 257**
Standing at King's Cross is Sturrock 251 Class no. 257. Stirling reboilered the class twice, first in the mid-1870s and again a decade later. No. 257 has the second slightly larger 4 ft 2½ in. diameter boiler here, whilst the previous type was 4 ft 0½ in. diameter. The locomotive was in service to January 1899.

Above **STURROCK 251 CLASS 2-4-0 NO. 251**
At the introduction of the 251 Class 2-4-0s, the engines were sent to sheds in the West Riding of Yorkshire for employment on intermediate express trains between locations in the area. After 15 years, several class members were displaced to other places, such as Hitchin. No. 251 was one of these and is pictured during the 1890s at an unidentified location. The locomotive was the first of the 251 Class erected by Sharp, Stewart & Co. in February 1866 and worked for the GNR to August 1899. No. 251 has the second Stirling boiler here, which was fitted in November 1889. The 251 Class survived to October 1902.

PATRICK STIRLING

Above and below **PATRICK STIRLING**
Gaining experience with several locomotive builders in the 1840s and 1850s, Patrick Stirling's first prominent appointment was the Locomotive Engineer of the Glasgow & South Western Railway in 1853. He served the company for 13 years before joining the GNR, initially as Doncaster Works Manager. He soon succeeded Sturrock and was with the GNR for 30 years. Above is a portrait of Stirling, c. 1880 and below he is central in a group consisting of the shop foremen at Doncaster Works in 1889.

Below STIRLING 0-4-2 NO. 18

When the line through Lincoln opened, the GNR established repair facilities for locomotives at Boston. When other sections of the route were ready for traffic, this was deemed too isolated from the network and plans were formulated to relocate to Peterborough. Chairman of the company Edmund Beckett Denison resided in Doncaster and championed the establishment of new workshops in the town. This occurred in the early 1850s, though around 15 years elapsed before the first locomotive was constructed there. Patrick Stirling became Locomotive Engineer in late 1866 and soon set about meeting goods traffic requirements with an 0-6-0, then for passenger services a 2-4-0 was provided. His third design fulfilled both of these roles and was an 0-4-2 based on a class he produced for his previous employers. The decision was made to erect the first of these 0-4-2s at Doncaster and no. 18 appeared in early 1868 with works no. 1. The engine is at Doncaster here before entering traffic.

Above STIRLING 0-4-2 NO. 77

Following on from Stirling's 0-4-2 no. 18 were six more locomotives to the design, all of which were erected at Doncaster in 1868. These proved successful and a steady stream of the engines appeared through to 1888, though there were some detail changes in this period. In 1873, six were added to the 34 already in service at that time. This batch and the previous one, consisting of five, had the benefit of slightly enlarged cylinders at 17½ in. diameter, compared to 17 in. originally. No. 77 was the product of Doncaster Works in December 1873 and has been caught here at King's Cross (the signage for the suburban station is just visible to the right) post-May 1887. At this date a 4 ft 2½ in. diameter boiler replaced the first slightly smaller one, whilst the driving wheel splashers have been enclosed, which was a modification from the early 1880s onwards, and the tender has coal rails fitted on the sides. The locomotive was condemned in November 1910.

STIRLING 0-4-2 NO. 570

Doncaster Works produced a steady stream of 0-4-2 locomotives through the early 1870s. At the mid-point of the decade, a large requirement for the type could not be fulfilled there and had to be contracted to Sharp, Stewart & Co. and Kitson & Co. for 30 and 20 engines respectively. No. 570 was built by the aforementioned in November 1876.

Above **STIRLING 0-4-2 NO. 11 – HATFIELD SHED**
At the time of the introduction of the Stirling 0-4-2, a shorter version, referred to as the 218 series, was built at Doncaster. Consisting of just four engines, no. 11 was amongst the number and is at Hatfield shed here in the late 1880s. Of note is the four-wheel tender which was paired to the engine from new.

Below **STIRLING 0-4-2 NO. 70**
Whereas the 218 series was shorter than standard engines, the 103 series had their size increased. Introduced in 1882, a total of 18 appeared from Doncaster up to the end of the decade, including no. 70 which was built there in November 1891. The locomotive is relatively new here as renumbering to 952 occurred in January 1892.

Opposite above STIRLING 126 CLASS 0-4-2WT NO. 131 – HADLEY WOOD

At the end of the 1860s, the London suburban services required reinforcements and Stirling adapted Sturrock's 0-4-2T design. A distinct visual change saw the outside frames moved inside, in addition to the bearings, though the rear axle remained with an outside arrangement, and a domeless boiler was fitted. After the first batch of two appeared in 1868, a second of four was completed in 1869, of which no. 131 was the last of this group. No. 131 has a southbound local train in the late 19th century.

Opposite below STIRLING 126 CLASS 0-4-2WT NO. 132 – EDGWARE

Further 0-4-2WT locomotives were built by Stirling in the early 1870s and numbered 13 when construction ceased. Known as the 126 Class, no. 132 was completed at Doncaster in 1870. The class was later rebuilt with a slightly larger diameter boiler and no. 132 was treated in June 1884. The engine is pictured at Edgware during the mid-1880s.

Below STIRLING F7 CLASS 0-4-2ST NO. 501

The GNR bypassed Stamford for an unknown reason when opening the main line and the Marquess of Exeter backed the Stamford & Essendine Railway to rectify this oversight. Initially worked by the GNR, the S&ER was obliged to work the line in the 1860s before the GNR again took the reins. Three 0-4-2T locomotives had been purchased but in the 1870s these were replaced by Stirling. Six 0-4-2ST engines were built at Doncaster, including no. 501 which is seen here at Essendine station. Initially known as the 501 Class, at the turn of the century the sextet was reclassified F7. No. 501 was in service until March 1913.

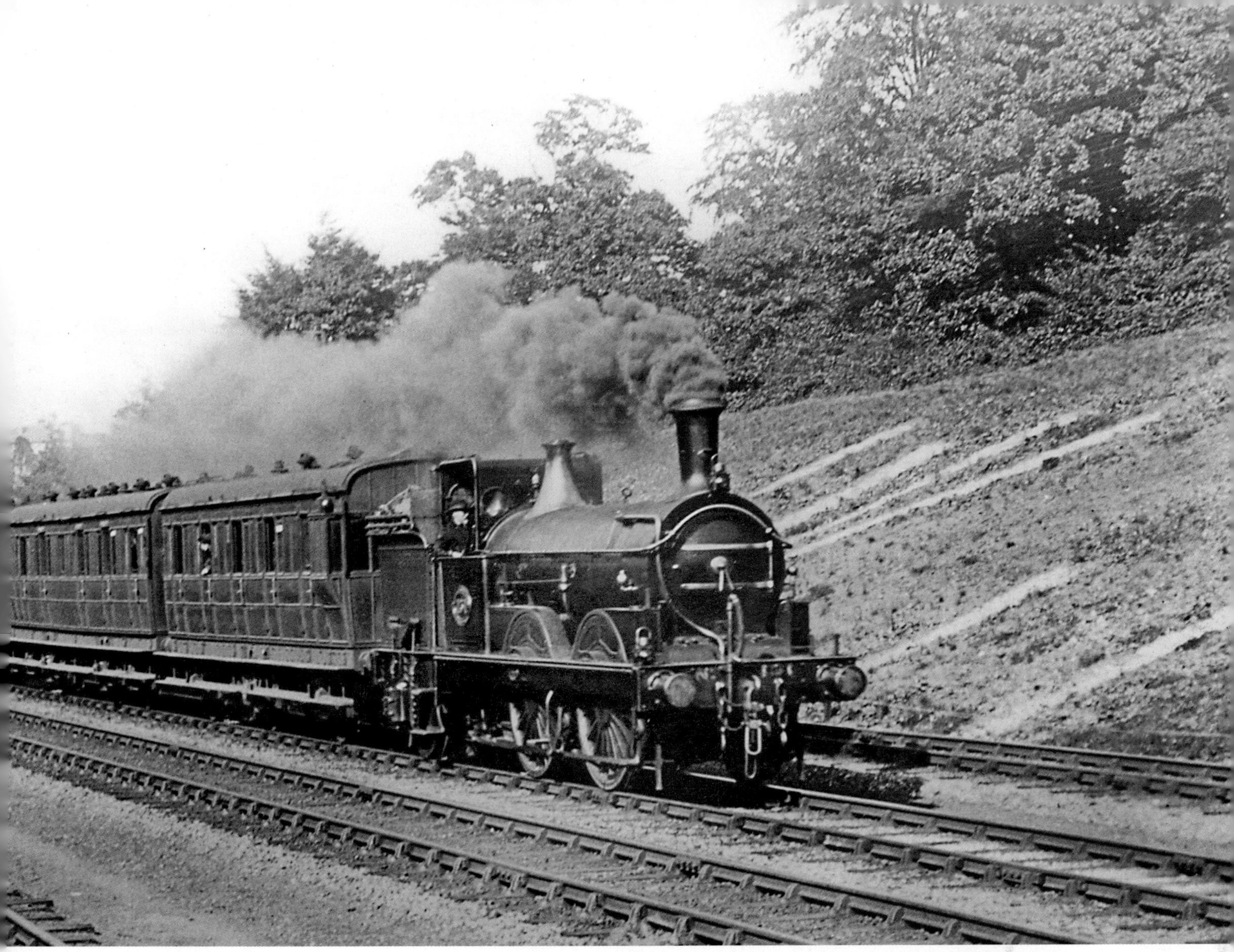

GREAT NORTHERN
132
RAILWAY

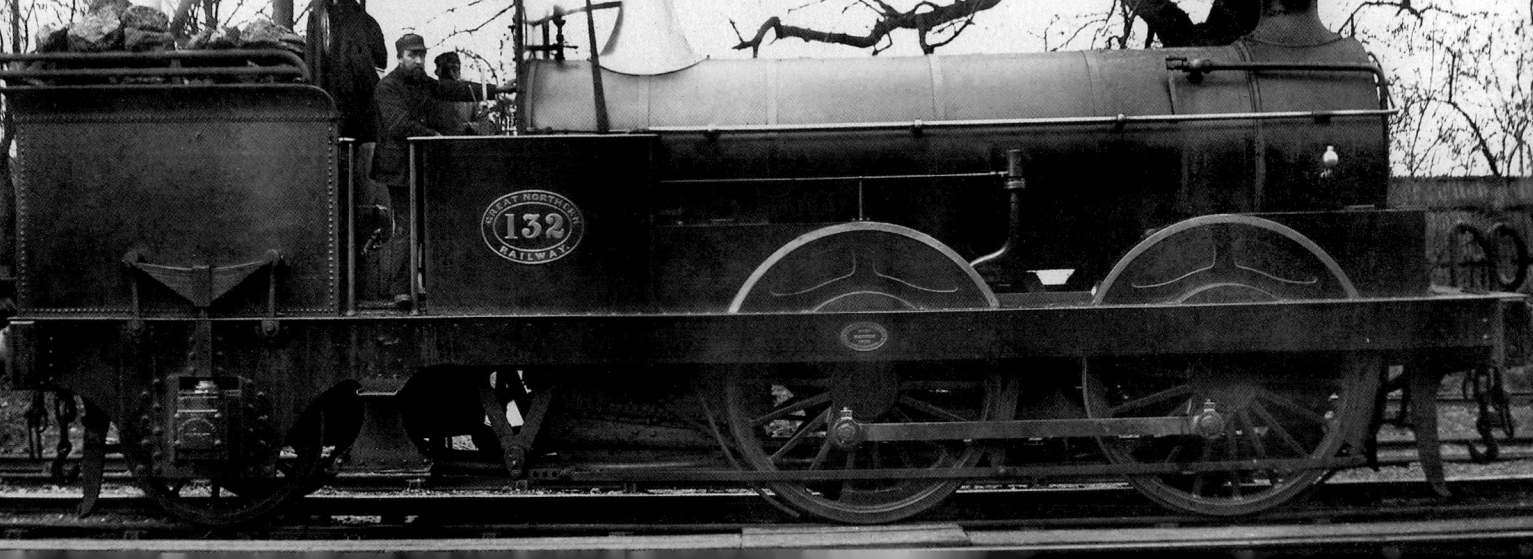

STIRLING 120 CLASS 0-4-4BT NO. 510 – EDGWARE

When more suburban locomotives were required, Stirling adopted a trailing bogie to provide a 0-4-4BT locomotive. The 0-4-2WT engines had a reputation for instability at the rear and the bogie was a remedy to this, as well as positioning the water tank at the rear (referred to as a 'back tank', or 'BT'). Otherwise, the 120 Class was relatively similar in other dimensions to the 126 Class. No. 510 was one of nine built at Doncaster Works in 1874. Many of this batch were delivered new to King's Cross and fitted with condensing apparatus. The locomotive poses with crew at Edgware in the mid-1890s. At this time a 4 ft 5 in. diameter boiler was fitted in place of the original 4 ft 0½ in. diameter type. No. 510 was in service to September 1907.

Above **STIRLING 658 CLASS 0-4-4T NO. 696**
Stirling moved to the side tank design in the early 1880s for suburban traffic. Ten built in 1884 and 1885 included no. 696, which is pictured. A total of 16 comprised the 658 0-4-4T Class.

Below **STIRLING 120 CLASS 0-4-4BT NO. 628 – KING'S CROSS**
In between duties at King's Cross is 120 Class 0-4-4BT no. 628. The locomotive entered traffic in September 1879 and was equipped with condensing gear when new. Since this time, a 4 ft 5 in. diameter boiler has been fitted.

STIRLING 206 CLASS 2-4-0 NO. 214 – HATFIELD

A freight train has been caught near Hatfield behind Stirling 206 Class 2-4-0 no. 214. The locomotive was built in September 1889 and in service to September 1908.

Above STIRLING 206 CLASS 2-4-0 NO. 755
Of the different variations of Stirling 2-4-0, the 206 Class was the most numerous, with over 70 erected in 11 years from 1884. The class covered several detail differences over earlier engines. No. 755 left Doncaster Works in November 1886 and was later rebuilt with an Ivatt 4 ft 5 in. domed boiler in 1904. The locomotive survived until just after Grouping.

Below STIRLING 78 CLASS 2-4-0 NO. 88
Face-to-face with Stirling 4-2-2 'Single' no. 1 is 78 Class 2-4-0 no. 88. The second member of the class built in 1882, these engines had a modified valve gear arrangement.

Opposite above **STIRLING 206 CLASS NO. 209 – YORK STATION**
The Great Northern Railway originally contemplated building their own line to York in the late 1840s. Yet, a mutually beneficial arrangement with the York & North Midland Railway to use each company's line between York and Doncaster was made and remained in force throughout the later realignments. Stirling 206 Class no. 209 has a passenger train at York station here. The locomotive was built at Doncaster in December 1884 and later received an Ivatt domed boiler in January 1907. This kept no. 209 active to November 1922.

Opposite below **STIRLING 206 CLASS NO. 87 – BELLE ISLE**
Just north of King's Cross station, between Gasworks and Copenhagen Tunnels, Stirling 206 Class 2-4-0 no. 87 is at Belle Isle with several other engines. Space and line capacities between the station and locomotive shed meant engines had to congregate at this point before being called to duty. No. 87 was constructed at Doncaster in June 1890 and in service to December 1912.

Below **STIRLING 223 CLASS 2-4-0 NO. 207**
Around the early 1880s, Stirling modified his standard boiler from 4 ft 0½ in. diameter to 4 ft 2½ in. The first 2-4-0s to be fitted with this from new was the 223 Class of 1880/1881. No. 207 was the third engine of the series completed at Doncaster by the end of the year. A local train has the locomotive at the head here passing an unidentified location.

Above **STIRLING 4-2-2 'SINGLE' NO. 5 – YORK STATION**
Following the initial prototype Stirling 4-2-2 'Single' engine, no. 1, two more experimental locomotives were built. These proved unsuccessful and Stirling reverted to the original arrangements for five which appeared over the first half of the 1870s. No. 5 was amongst these and in traffic from August 1873. The locomotive's driver poses in the cab here at York station. Photograph from the David P. Williams Colour Archive.

Above **STIRLING 4-2-2 'SINGLE' NO. 221 – KING'S CROSS STATION**
In 1876 two 'Singles' were built and these had the trailing wheels increased 6 in. to 4 ft 7 in. diameter. No. 221 was the first of the pair and is pictured at King's Cross station. The locomotive was new to Peterborough and worked between King's Cross and York. Of interest on the buffer beam is the cylinder bore and stroke (18 x 28 in.) information which sits above the number.

Below **STIRLING 4-2-2 'SINGLE' NO. 95 – POTTERS BAR**
Stirling 716 Class 0-6-0 no. 748 is passed by 'Single' no. 95 which has a train of passenger carriages at Potters Bar. The latter was built in 1880 with an altered cab design which became standard.

STIRLING 4-2-2 'SINGLE' NO. 48

No. 48 was built at Doncaster in October 1874 and had been in service for little over a year when involved with the Abbots Ripton rail crash. This occurred on 21st January 1876 during a snowstorm. A coal train being shunted at Abbots Ripton station was run into by the southbound 'Flying Scotsman' due to signalling confusion, which was further compounded by slow reactions of signalmen following the crash. This allowed a Leeds express to collide with the carriages and wagons. A total of 13 died and 59 were injured. No. 48 was repaired and returned to service, being withdrawn in 1908.

Above **STIRLING 4-2-2 'SINGLE' NO. 53**
No. 53 was part of a group of four 'Singles' built in 1875/1876 that had the boiler pitch raised 1½ in. to 7 ft 2½ in. The locomotive was also the first of the type allocated to King's Cross which is interesting as several were in traffic by this time. Mainly working from Peterborough and Doncaster, Grantham and Leeds also shared in the class members. No. 53 is seen in more rural, unidentified surroundings here.

Below **STIRLING 4-2-2 'SINGLE' NO. 93**
No. 93 was the first 'Single' to have the cab side lengthened by 3 in. and this was perpetuated thereafter. For the engine and no. 95 following, the number of boiler tubes was also reduced.

Above **DONCASTER CRIMPSALL WORKSHOPS**
Work on the structure for the Crimpsall repair shop progresses in late 1900. As seen, standard gauge lines were laid to help move materials around the site, including an extremely large number of bricks used for both the walls and drainage works (on the right). When completed, an 18 in.-gauge system was installed inside the repair shop to move equipment and materials. In the distance, the Tender Shop can be glimpsed.

Above **DONCASTER CRIMPSALL WORKSHOPS**
View north east to the original works site from the Crimpsall Repair Shop in 1900. The steel support members are in the midst of being positioned and these appear to have been at least partially supplied by Phoenix Foundry, Derby, which is painted on several beams on the left. Founded in 1834, the company supplied ironwork for a number of railway projects, such as bridges, stations, etc.

Below **DONCASTER CRIMPSALL WORKSHOPS**
Some of the ironwork for the Crimpsall Repair shop stands in position during 1899. A steam crane is also lifting a beam in the centre, whilst off to the right progress has been made completing the frontage for the Tender Shop.

Above **DONCASTER CRIMPSALL WORKSHOPS**
Even though much of the Repair Shop building is not yet complete, a start has been made on the roof during 1899. Timber beams (presumably for this) have been assembled in what became the yard here and are interestingly loaded on pairs of 9-ton single bolster wagons branded 'Cheshire Lines'.

Below **DONCASTER CRIMPSALL WORKSHOPS**
When completed, the Crimpsall Repair Shop had four bays that were 520 ft long by 52 ft wide and two smaller bays 520 ft by 30 ft. The latter were used by coppersmiths and fitters to carry out machining as well as minor boiler repairs. The four repair bays were served by two 35-ton capacity overhead cranes.

Above and below **DONCASTER WORKS PAINT SHOP**
H. Arnold & Son were employed on the building work for the whole Crimpsall construction project and this eventually cost the GNR £250,000. The Paint Shop was on the eastern side of the site. Eight roads with shallow pits were provided, each being able to hold five engines. Two views of the building under construction are reproduced here.

Above and below **DONCASTER WORKS TENDER SHOP**

At the rear of the Crimpsall Repair Shop, a new Tender Shop was built. This had two bays containing three tracks each with space for a total of 32 tenders and a smaller bay where machine tools were placed. In the bottom image, the rear of the Tender Shop is depicted, whilst in the distance is the Crimpsall, with the Wheel Shop connected at the rear.

GNR WORKFORCE

Above **DONCASTER WEST CARRIAGE SHOP**
When the Wagon Shops were removed to Doncaster Carr, the Carriage Department filled the remaining space. Also, additional buildings were provided at the edge of the site on the bank of the River Don. These were the North Carriage Shed and West Carriage Shop. In the latter, which was devoted to repair operations, on 20th March 1913, two workers are engaged moving a wheelset with a 'wheel pinch'. This dangerous-looking method was later superseded by Simpson's patent 'wheel swivel' which moved the wheels by the axle centre. Michael Harris in *Gresley's Coaches* notes that at this time carriage wheelsets were supplied by Cravens Carriage & Wagon Co. Ltd, Sheffield.

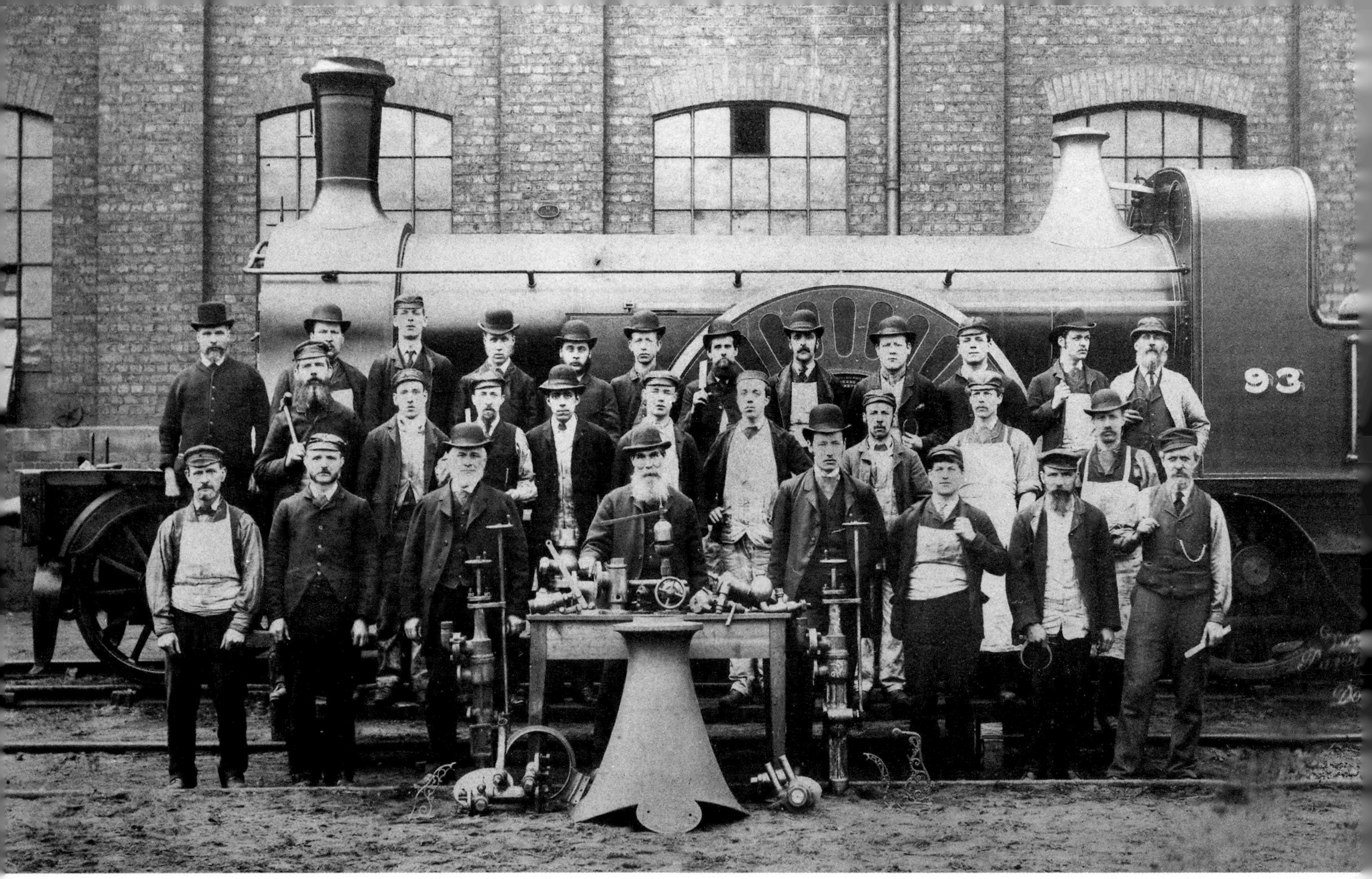
93

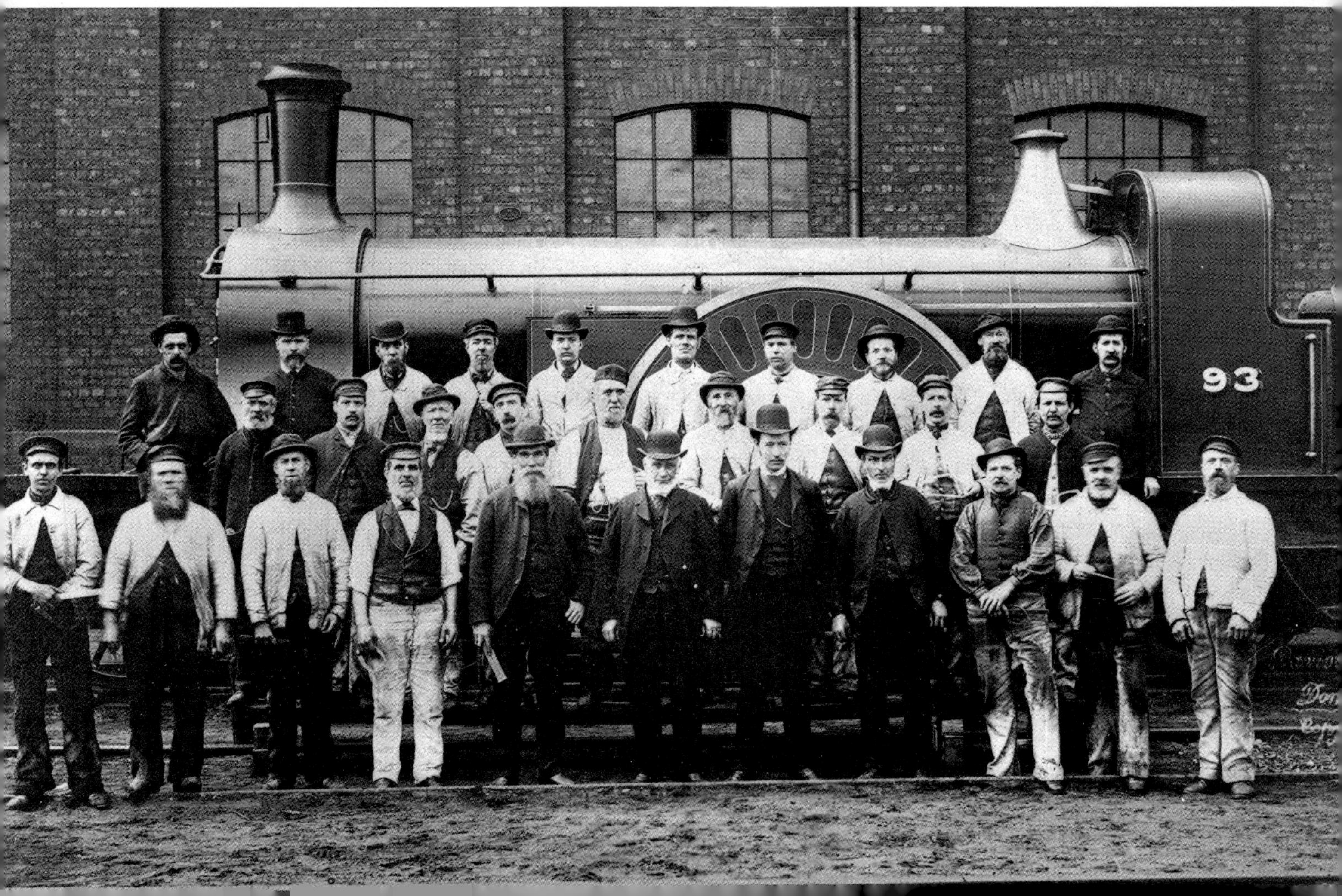
93

Above **DONCASTER WORKS**
One of the tasks in finishing a coupling rod is skilfully carried out at Doncaster Works by two men under the watchful eye of a foreman, likely at the turn of the century.

Opposite above and below **DONCASTER WORKS STAFF WITH STIRLING 4-2-2 'SINGLE' NO. 93**
During May 1887, employees at Doncaster Works have broken from their duties to take these two group portraits in front of Stirling 4-2-2 'Single' no. 93. Above, the Brass Finishers have the components they work on in front of them, including the safety valve cover, whistle, valves, gauges and works plate, whilst below are Fitters and Turners from the Upper Turnery. No. 93 was constructed at Doncaster in December 1879 and employed by the GNR to May 1906. A Stirling 4 ft 2 in. diameter boiler was fitted in October 1889 and the engine later had an Ivatt domed boiler from June 1896. At the latter date, the locomotive was employed at Grantham.

G.N.R
Brass Finishers
DONCASTER

Above **DONCASTER CRIMPSALL REPAIR SHOP**
A scene captured inside the Crimpsall Repair Shop during the early 20th century. On the right is Stirling J52 Class 0-6-0ST no. 1207.

Opposite above **DONCASTER WORKS, BRASS FINISHERS**
A new Brass Foundry was built at Doncaster in the mid-1860s. Located near the Boiler Shop, the building contained 12 crucible hearths. In the 1890s, the Upper Turnery, which was in the main building fronting on to Doncaster station, had around 50 men engaged on work readying brass for use on the locomotives (carriages also used brass components and space for this was later provided at the North Carriage Shed). Many of these men – and boys in the front row – have gathered for this group portrait to be taken around the turn of the century.

Opposite below **DONCASTER WORKS MACHINE SHOP**
Men are busy in several tasks in the Machine Shop at Doncaster Works, c. 1900. Much of the machining was done in the Upper and Lower Turneries from the opening of Doncaster Works to the 1930s when all the equipment was removed to the original Erecting and Tender Shops.

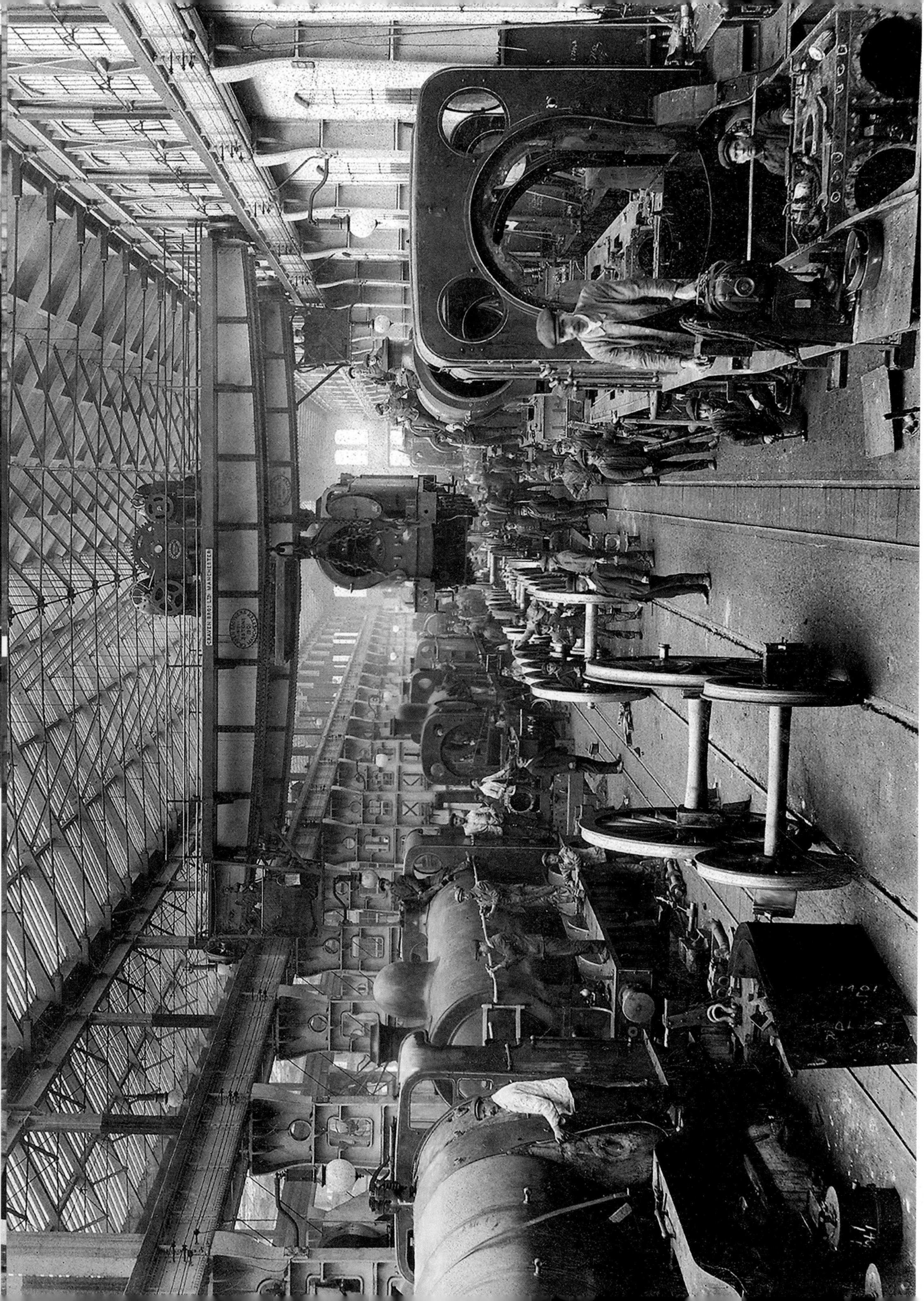

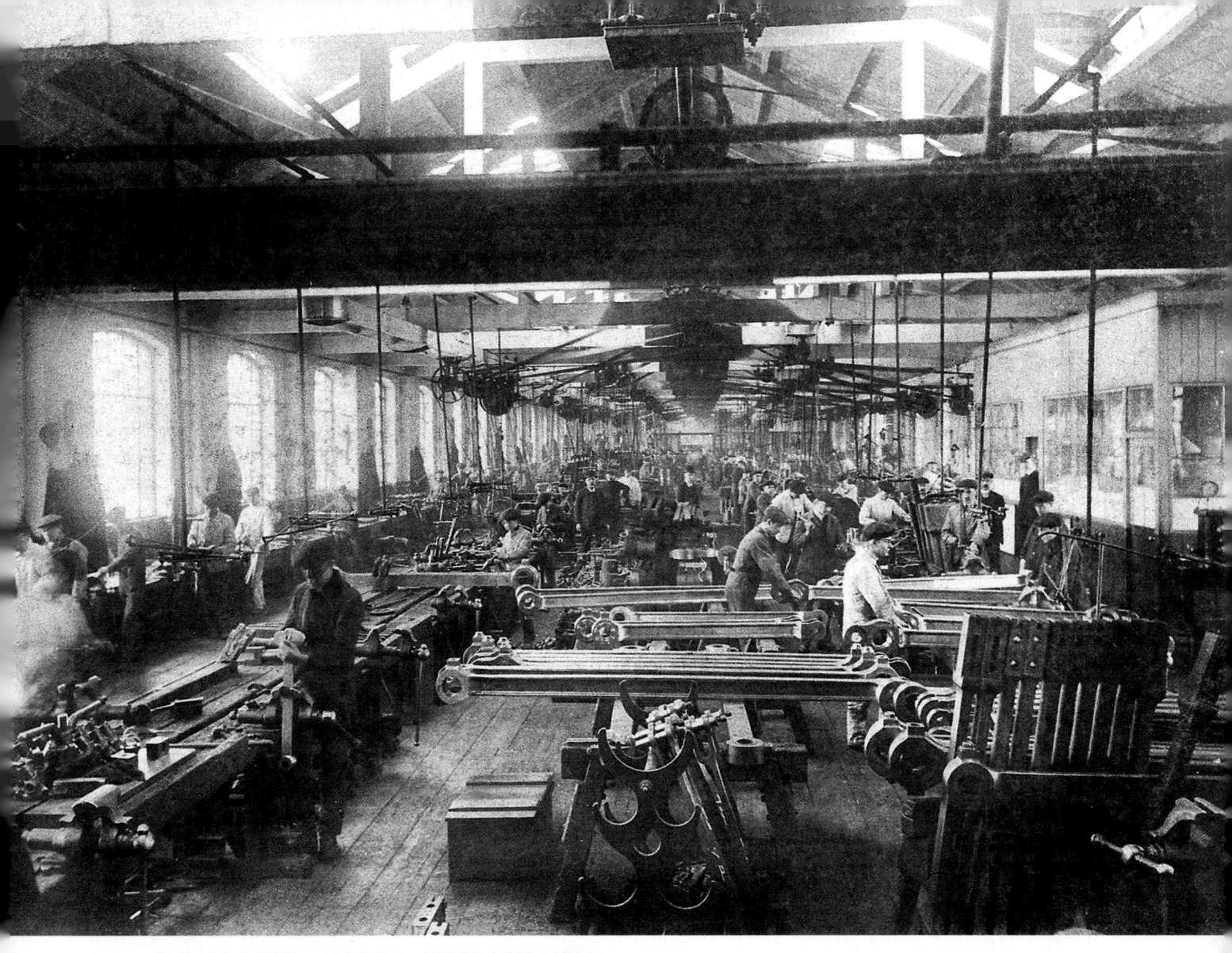

Above **DONCASTER WORKS UPPER TURNERY**
A number of connecting rods are in the Upper Turnery for machining, c. 1900. Employing around 200 people at the time, the shop contained several specialised tools for machining case-hardened metal, as well as making cotter holes.

Opposite **DONCASTER WORKS CRIMPSALL REPAIR SHOP**
When the Crimpsall Repair Shop opened in the early 20th century, there were six total bays in use and four were for the repair of locomotives. These were 520 ft long by 52 ft wide and had a total capacity of 100 locomotives. As seen, there were two bays per section of the building, with each served by a 35-ton capacity overhead crane, whilst two sets of 18-in. rail lines were in use for the movement of materials. Identifiable on the left is Ivatt C1 'Large Boiler' 4-4-2 'Atlantic' locomotive no. 1401 which was constructed at Doncaster in June 1905. The engine is in the Crimpsall five years later and has an Ivatt K1 Class 0-8-0 stood behind.

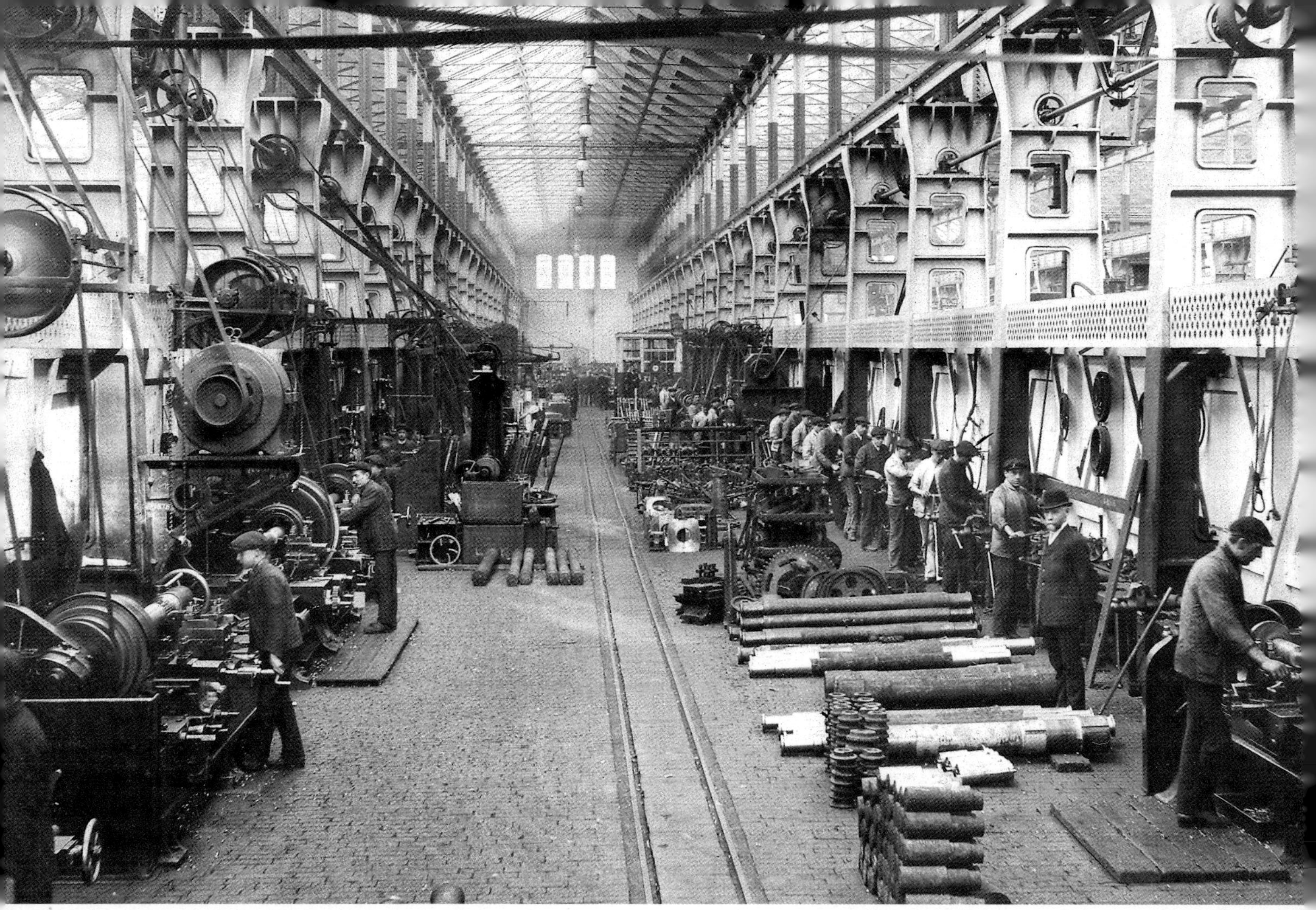

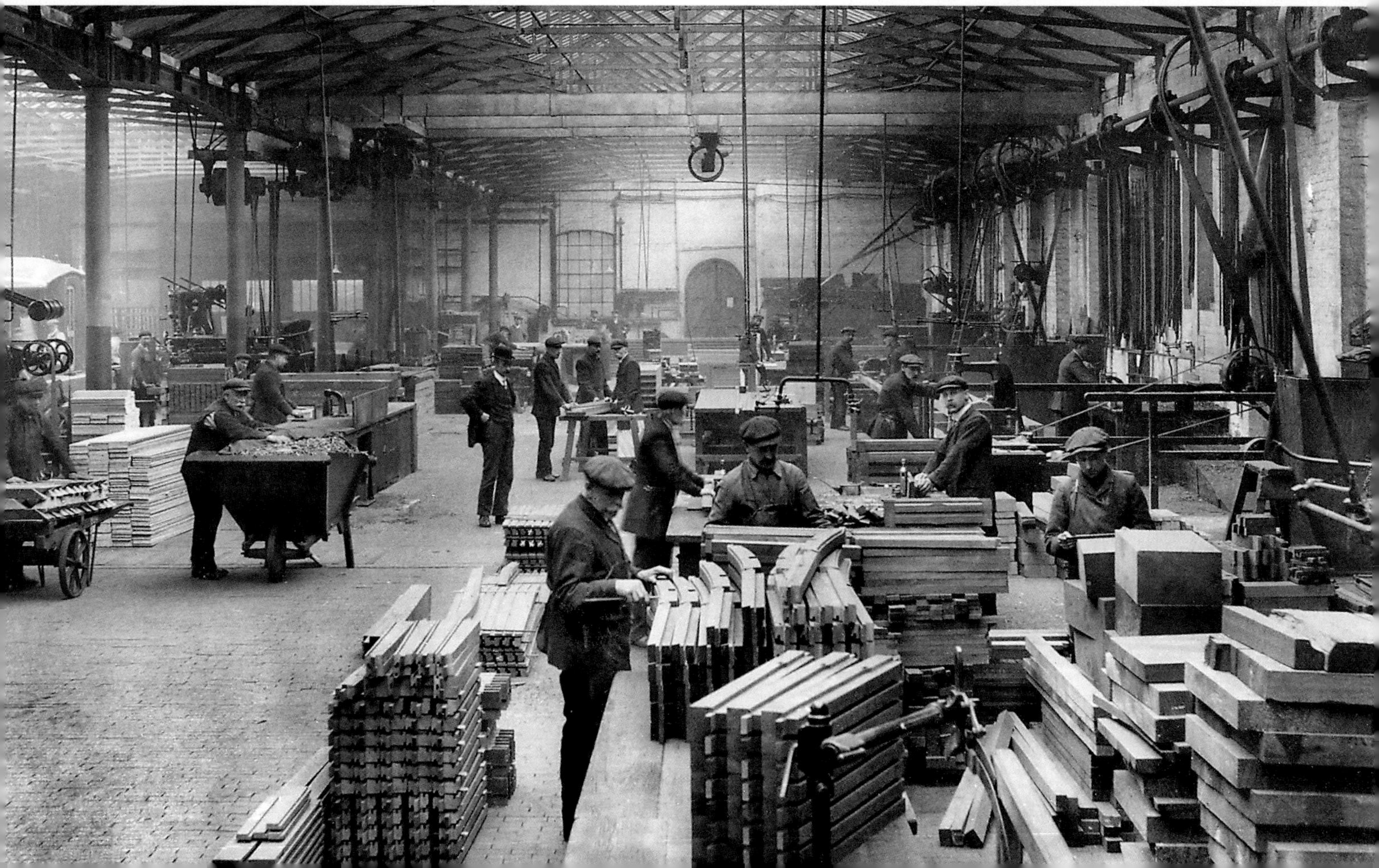

Above **DONCASTER WAGON WORKS PAINT SHOP**
A small shop at Doncaster Carr Wagon Works was dedicated to painting the wagons in the standard GNR livery. This was black running gear with red oxide sides, whilst refrigerator vehicles had white sides. Lettering was white on the first mentioned and black on the latter and the stencil for doing this is visible here in this scene captured in the mid-1910s.

Opposite above **DONCASTER WORKS CRIMPSALL REPAIR SHOP**
Supporting the repair bays in the Crimpsall were two smaller 30-ft wide machine bays. These were mainly populated by coppersmiths and boilersmiths to carry out minor repairs. Both compressed air and electric tools were in use.

Opposite below **DONCASTER WORKS CARRIAGE SHOP**
At the southern end of the Carriage Shop an area was given over to various woodworking tools, such as band saws, drills, circular saws and planers. A view of this area has been captured in the early 1920s.

Above **DONCASTER WORKS CRIMPSALL REPAIR SHOP**
Fitters in the Crimpsall's 1-Bay pause their work to pose for this image taken in the early 20th century. Note the small boiler tubes loaded in the wagon on the 18-in. gauge line. One of the first points when entering the repair shop was to determine the boiler condition as this could cause the engine to be delayed there.

Above **DONCASTER WORKS NEW ERECTING SHOP**
A batch of Ivatt's C1 Class 'Atlantics' are under construction in the New Erecting Shop.

Below **DONCASTER WORKS TENDER SHOP STAFF**
A group photograph of workers from the Tender Shop, c. 1908.

64   THE GLORIOUS YEARS OF THE GNR – GNR WORKFORCE

Above **DONCASTER WORKS STAFF**
A group of fitters have their portrait taken in front of the Crimpsall Repair Shop during the early 20th century.

Opposite above **DONCASTER WORKS CRIMPSALL REPAIR SHOP**
As mentioned, 100 locomotives could be accommodated in the Crimpsall Repair Shop. One would arrive on the centre road and be partially stripped before being removed from the wheelsets and placed in one of the spare bays. There, the engine was completely dismantled. The parts were assessed and delivered to the various areas of the works for refurbishment or replacement before arriving back for reassembly. In the early 20th century, the time an engine spent in Doncaster Works averaged 60 days. Several locomotives could be under attention by the gangs and overseen by a charge-hand. In the 1930s, rationalisations were carried out which reduced repair times by just over half. This view of 1-Bay in the Crimpsall was taken in 1912/1913.

Opposite below **DONCASTER WORKS BLACKSMITHS**
In addition to the Forge, there was also a Smithy at Doncaster Works. This contained 40 double hearths and 80 anvils where some of the smaller locomotive items were created and worked on. A steam hammer was also present. In the late 19th century, the workers were paid according to productivity and some worked in groups which were kept the same to ensure a close relationship. A group of blacksmiths is seen here.

Above **DONCASTER WORKS BRASS FOUNDRY**
The Brass Foundry originally operated in the Forge, though in a round of modernisations in the late 19th century a dedicated building was erected near the Boiler Shop. The Brass Foundry had 12 crucible hearths arranged at a suitable height for manoeuvrability, whilst the building had ample light sources for work to progress quickly and safely. Items are being cast here in the Foundry during late 1907.

WAGON WORKS

Above **DONCASTER CARR WAGON WORKS**
In the early days of the company, the GNR duplicated locomotive practice to carriage and wagons as vehicles were purchased – or rented – from the trade and repairs carried out when necessary. With the establishment of Doncaster Works, a dedicated area was given over to the Wagon Department and construction of new wagons later began. In the 1880s, the Wagon shops were removed from Doncaster Works to Doncaster Carr which was a short distance to the south on the western side of the East Coast Main Line. Work on the new shops was completed in the late 1880s by local firm H. Arnold & Son for a price around £25,000. This overview of the Carr Wagon Works was taken on 8th May 1908 and a number of wagon types, new and old, are in the yard.

Above IVATT K1 CLASS 0-8-0 NO. 453
The GNR favoured 0-6-0 locomotives for goods and mineral traffic. As an increase in train capacity was deemed desirable in the late 1890s, Ivatt devised an 0-8-0 capable of hauling over 50 10-ton wagons, whereas the limit previously had been in the mid-30s. The new design – classified K1 – had a prototype created at Doncaster in February 1901. This was proved more than capable leading to further orders. The last ten of the 55 built in total appeared during 1909 and five of these had superheaters, as well as piston valves from new. No. 453 was amongst this group and completed by November 1909. The locomotive has a loaded coal train here in the mid-1910s.

Below **IVATT N1 CLASS 0-6-2T NO. 1569**
A feature peculiar to N1 Class nos 1561-1570 was the size of the rear, circular windows. The standard for the class was 1 ft 6 in. diameter whereas the aforementioned had 1 ft 2 in. diameter windows from new. These were protected from stray coal pieces by four bars which can be glimpsed here to the left of the second gentleman in the cab, who is likely the driver. The other N1s had five metal bars owing to the larger diameter screens. No. 1569 was built at Doncaster in May 1910 and sent to London for the suburban traffic – condensing apparatus is fitted here.

Above **IVATT K1 CLASS 0-8-0 NO. 404**
Shortly after Gresley's appointment as Locomotive Engineer, tests began on the use of a feedwater heater fitted to Ivatt K1 Class 0-8-0 no. 439. This was of the Weir type and a second was given to no. 440 which was also superheated. The aim of this equipment was to use exhaust steam to preheat water before entering the boiler, therefore saving energy. The Weir type was later removed from both locomotives and in June 1917 another experiment in this area began with no. 404 acquiring a Willans heater with Worthington pump. The latter is seen on the running plate of no. 404 in this picture. Though this was also stripped from the engine subsequently, Gresley persisted with the technology into the 1920s and 1930s. He also continued to find similarly unsatisfactory results.

Below **IVATT K1 CLASS 0-8-0 NO. 425**
As the last K1s were being built with superheaters, thoughts turned to equipping the earlier engines with the apparatus. This occurred in the early 1910s and no. 425 received a Schmidt superheater in June 1913. Many of these were also given balanced slide valves at the same time which was the case for no. 425. The locomotive is at the head of a loaded coal train near Potters Bar.

Above IVATT K1 CLASS 0-8-0 NO. 417
A train of unloaded coal wagons is with K1 no. 417 in the early 1900s. The locomotive was built at Doncaster in January 1903 and went on to be the first GNR superheated locomotive when equipped in late 1908 – piston valves were also used.

Below IVATT K1 CLASS 0-8-0 NO. 418 AND NO. 419
Awaiting admission to the Crimpsall Repair Shop on 1st July 1909 are two Ivatt K1 Class 0-8-0s, nos 418 and 419. These were six years old at this point and the first mentioned went on to be superheated in 1914. No. 419 never received the alterations and was condemned in 1928, though no. 418 was withdrawn in the following year.

IVATT L1 CLASS 0-8-2T NO. 144

A large number of Ivatt's L1 Class 0-8-2T locomotives congregated at Colwick shed, Nottingham, for work on local coal trains and shunting. No. 144 was amongst this group and is pictured at Colwick here. The engine was in service from August 1906 to August 1930.

Above **IVATT L1 CLASS 0-8-2T NO. 117**
Suburban traffic was the original purpose for the Ivatt L1 Class 0-8-2T, yet the design soon proved unsuitable and their subsequent role in the capital was limited. No. 117 was the first of the production engines built at Doncaster Works in October 1904 and has a northbound suburban train from King's Cross here.

Below **IVATT L1 CLASS 0-8-2T NO. 152**
A group pose with Ivatt L1 Class no. 152 at what is thought to be Ardsley shed around 1906/1907. The engine was new to the depot, though all class members transferred from the West Riding to Colwick in the early 1910s.

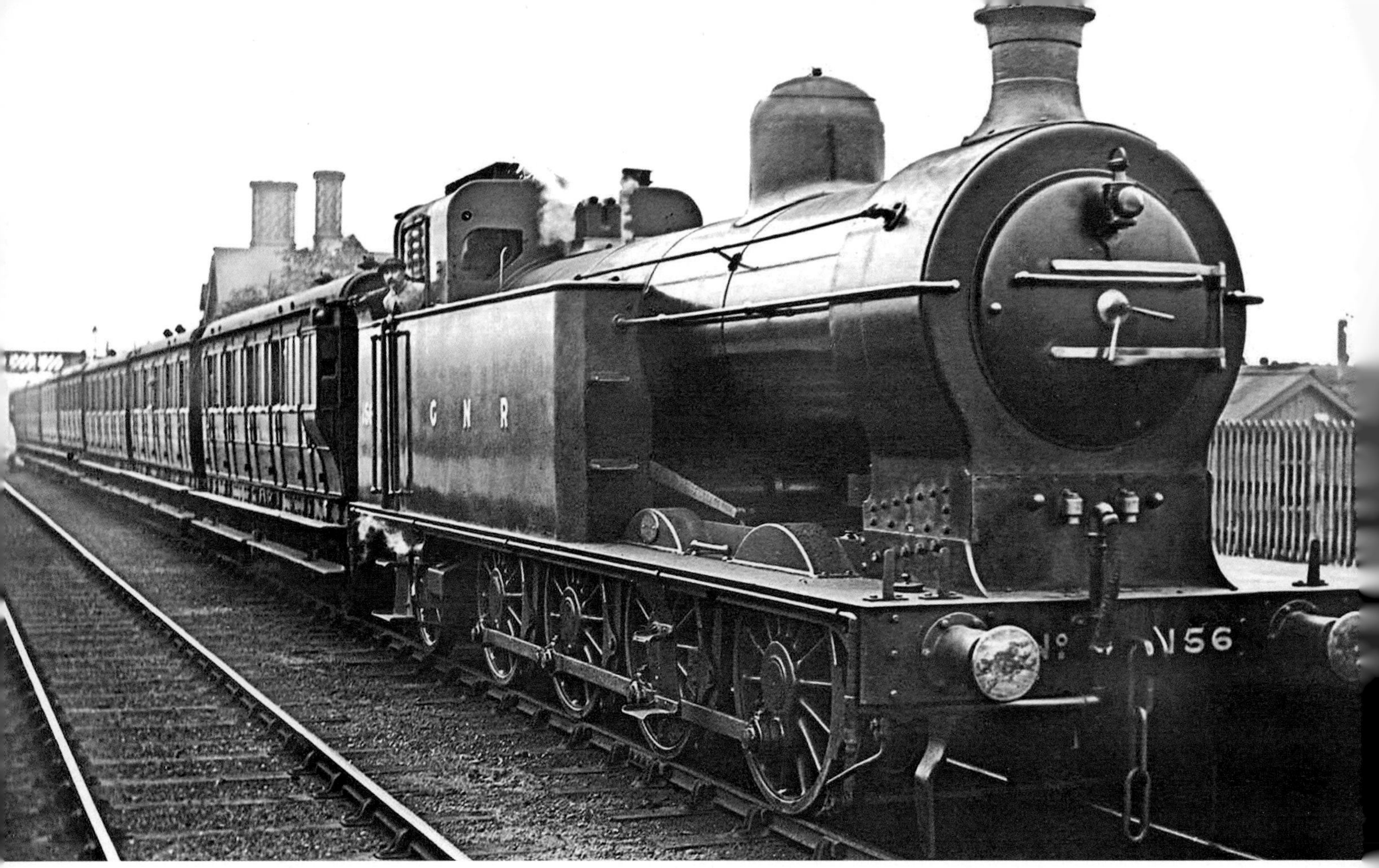
G N R

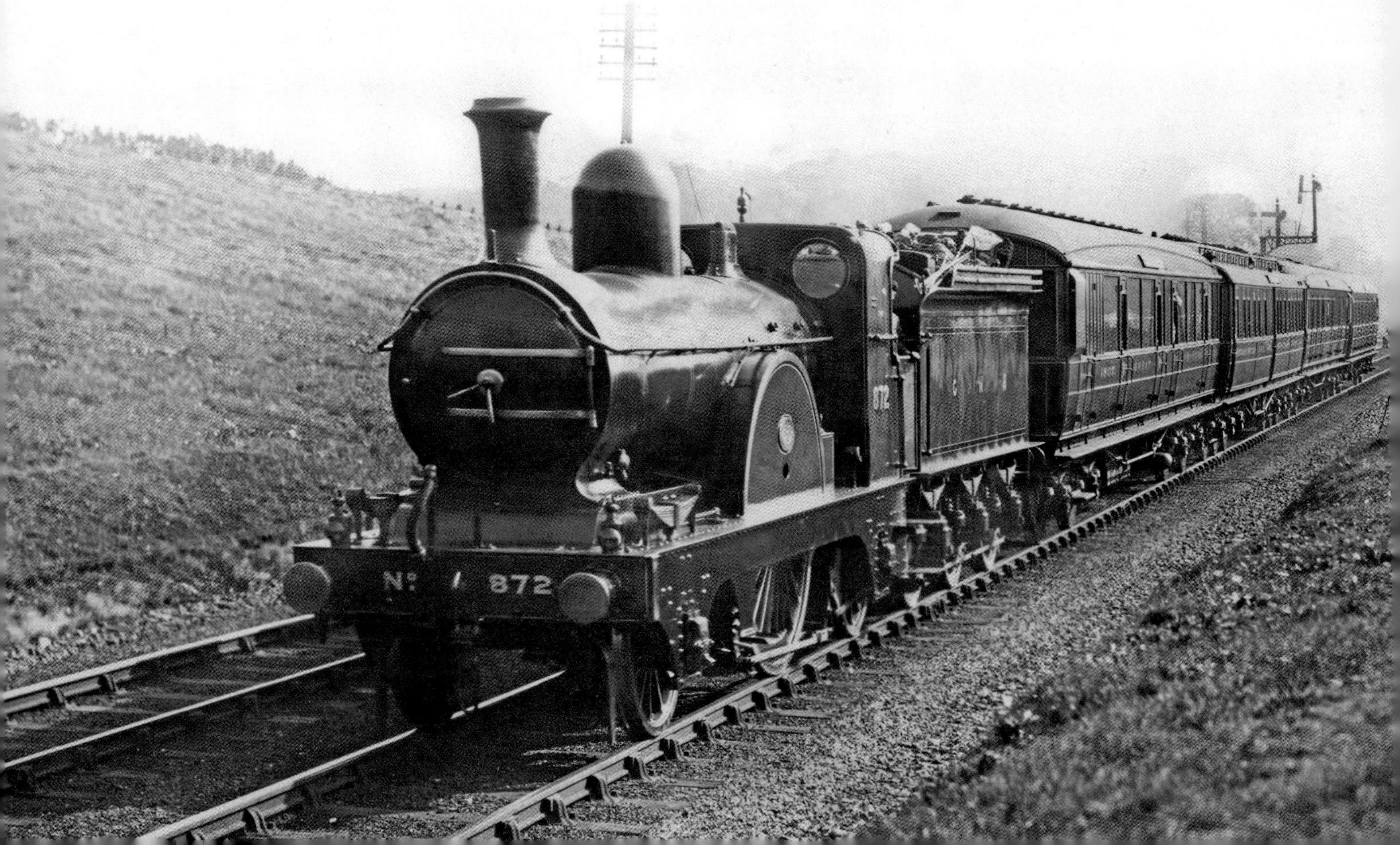

Above **STIRLING 2-2-2 'SINGLE' NO. 873**
One of the first Stirling 7 ft 6 in. 'Singles' rebuilt with an Ivatt domed boiler was no. 873. Another change at this time concerned the cab which was slightly modified. No. 873 worked in London for many years and was withdrawn in September 1911.

Opposite above **IVATT L1 CLASS 0-8-2T NO. 156**
The GNR took steps to break the stranglehold of the Midland Railway in the Nottingham area from the late 1860s. A route to Nottingham from Grantham already existed as the Ambergate, Nottingham, Boston & Eastern Junction Railway was absorbed in the late 1850s, yet the GNR sought to extend to Derby, Burton upon Trent and Stafford. This project was completed in stages throughout the 1870s, with the first reaching northward to Pinxton for the transport of coal from local collieries in 1875. On 1st February 1876 passenger services were provided and one of the stations on the line was New Basford station. Soon afterwards the name was changed to Basford & Bullwell which remained in use to the early 1950s when becoming Basford North. Ivatt L1 Class no. 156 has a local train at the station during the early 20th century. The locomotive was originally new to Bradford when completed as the last class member in December 1906. At Colwick, the L1s mainly operated coal trains, though could find employment on miners' passenger trains.

Opposite below **STIRLING 2-2-2 'SINGLE' NO. 872**
Several Stirling 7 ft 6 in. 'Singles' were given new 4 ft 2 in. domed boilers by Ivatt in the late 1890s, though a plan to provide a new leading bogie was discarded. No. 872 first received the boiler in May 1901, when nearly ten years old, and this had a slightly larger grate area than a second Ivatt boiler carried from May 1910. The locomotive was in service for another three years subsequently.

THE GLORIOUS YEARS OF THE GNR – H.A. IVATT

IVATT E1 CLASS 2-4-0 NO. 1066
No. 1066 was built at Doncaster in April 1897 and in service to July 1921.

Above **STIRLING 206 CLASS 2-4-0 NO. 867**
In May 1898 no. 867, of Stirling's 206 Class, was given an Ivatt 4 ft 5 in. diameter domed boiler. This is carried by the locomotive here as a train is hauled through Potters Bar & South Mimms station. An Ivatt 4-4-0 is the train engine.

Below **STIRLING 206 CLASS 2-4-0 NO. 883**
Another double-headed train is seen, in this instance as Ganwick. 206 Class no. 883 with Ivatt boiler is coupled to D1 Class 4-4-0 no. 1388.

Below **IVATT C1 CLASS 'LARGE' 4-4-2 'ATLANTIC' NO. 1449**

Activity at Doncaster station briefly pauses as the Royal train passes through behind Ivatt C1 no. 1449 in the early 20th century. The locomotive appeared from Doncaster in August 1908, at which time the GNR was also assembling a Royal train for King Edward VII. Shortly after being completed, no. 1449 was involved with exchange trials with the London & North Western Railway which saw a member of George Whale's 'Precursor' Class 4-4-0 compete against Ivatt's 'Atlantic'. No. 1449 ran between Euston and Crewe for a week in 1909 and managed to show a slight economy over the LNWR engine. A similar result occurred on the GNR main line.

Above **IVATT C1 CLASS 'LARGE' 4-4-2 'ATLANTIC' NO. 1451**
A local housing development resulted in the opening of Oakleigh Park station, around eight miles from King's Cross station. This occurred in early December 1873, though by the end of the century a replacement station had been built owing to an increase in running lines. Ivatt C1 Class no. 1451 was the last of ten constructed at Doncaster during 1908 and had entered traffic by August.

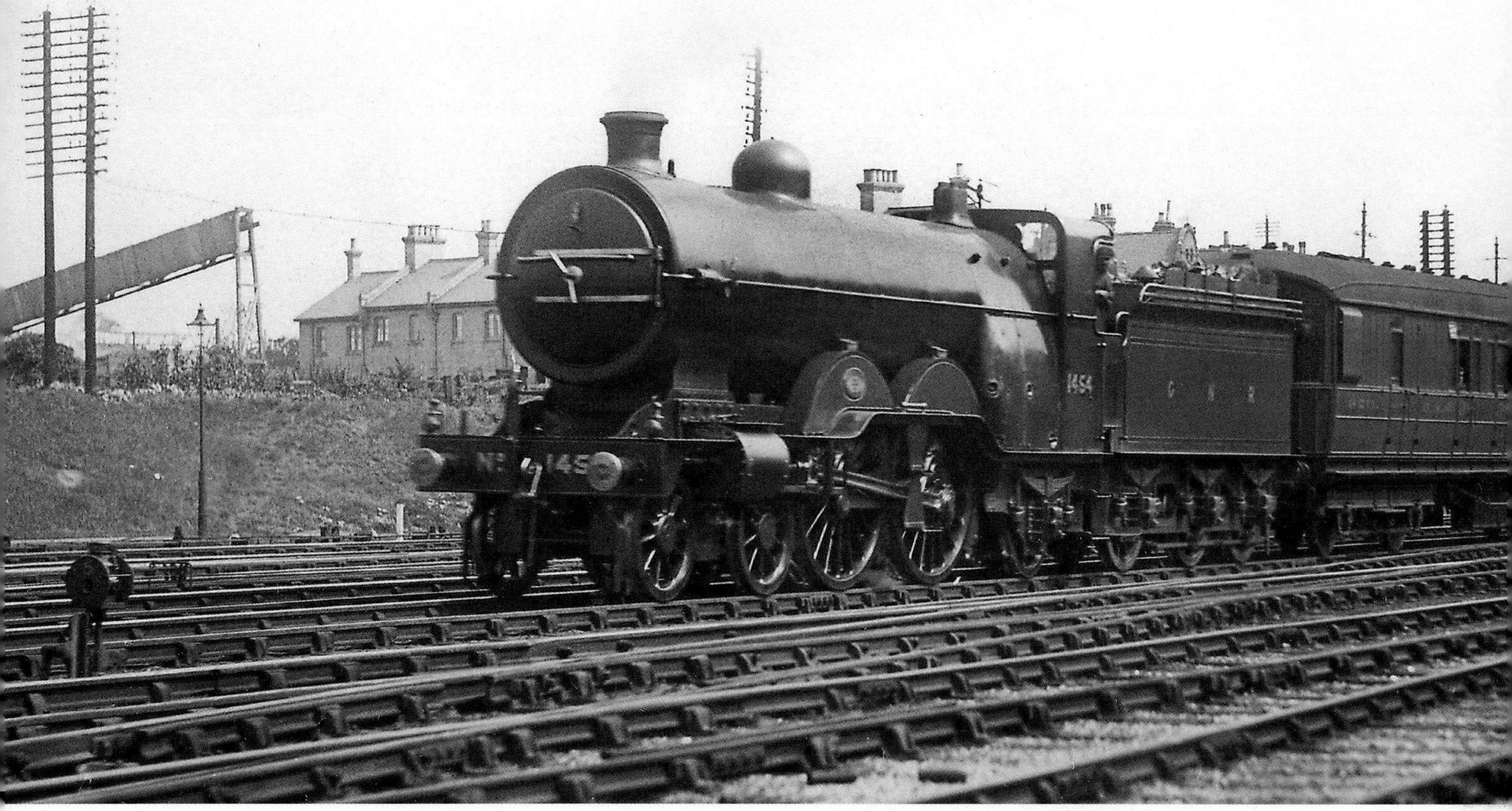
1454
G N R

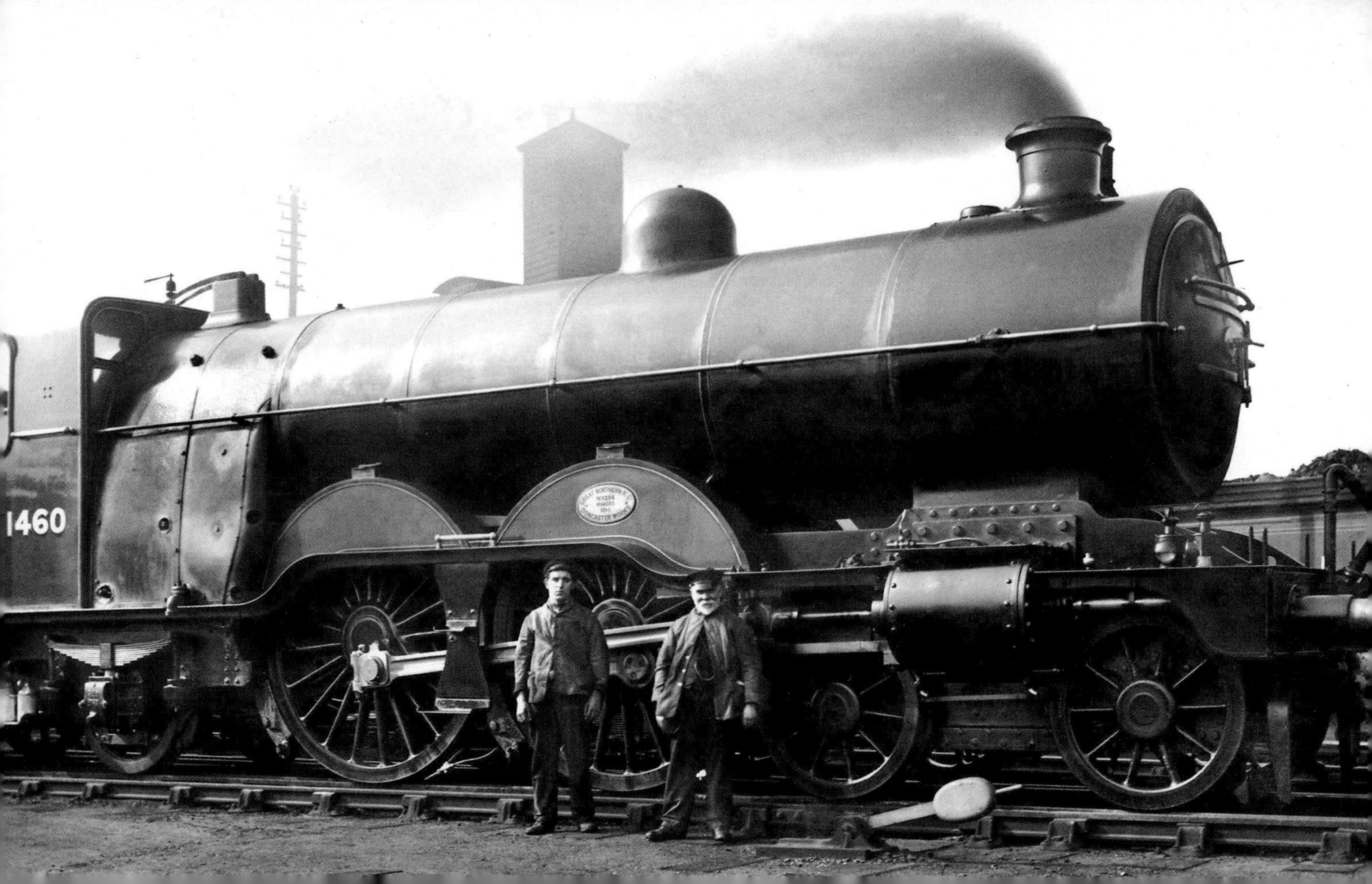
1460

Opposite above **IVATT C1 CLASS 'LARGE' 4-4-2 'ATLANTIC' NO. 1454**
As the first decade of the 20th century came to an end, the use of a superheater in a locomotive's boiler gained increasing popularity. Ivatt was influenced and installed a Schmidt 18-element superheater in several 0-8-0s, as well as C1 no. 988. This was successful enough for the final ten 'Atlantics' ordered in 1910 – which brought the class total to 116 (including both types) – to have 18-element superheaters from new. No. 1454 was amongst this group and was built in September. As superheaters were unsuitable with slide valves, these 10 'Atlantics' also had piston valves which were 8 in. diameter.

Opposite below **IVATT C1 CLASS 'LARGE' 4-4-2 'ATLANTIC' NO. 1460**
The penultimate Ivatt 'Atlantic', no. 1460, stands here behind the crew, who pause briefly for this image to be captured in the early 20th century. The locomotive was in traffic for November 1910 and as well as having the superheater and piston valves, slightly larger cylinders – 20 in. by 24 in. stroke – were fitted. This was the case for the other ten engines of the order.

Below **IVATT J21 CLASS 0-6-0 NO. 8**
Several of Stirling's 0-6-0 goods locomotives were rebuilt under Ivatt and towards the end of his tenure, he decided to introduce a small number of new engines for express goods duties. These had 5 ft 8 in. diameter wheels and 15 were erected initially. No. 8 was part of the order and completed at Doncaster in October 1908. Despite having an intended role on freight services, no. 8 has a passenger train at Oakleigh Park station and this was the case for London-based J21 Class locomotives.

Above IVATT J5 CLASS 0-6-0 NO. 1136
Ten Stirling 4 ft 7 in. 0-6-0 goods locomotives were being built at the time of his death. Ivatt decided to continue with the design and a further 133 appeared to the turn of the century. His main alteration was the provision of a domed boiler and cast-iron safety valve cover, along with other small changes. No. 1136 was amongst 25 built at Kitson & Co. in 1900 and these were in turn part of the larger 343 series denoting differences over earlier engines, including moved sandboxes, whilst the Kitson engines also had cast-iron chimneys.

Opposite above IVATT J5 CLASS 0-6-0 NO. 318
Preceding the 343 series of the J5 Class was the 315 series and these had redesigned cabs from pre-August 1898 engines when they first appeared. Modifications were also made to the frames and brakes at this time, as well as small details such as the footsteps. No. 318 was built at Doncaster during the aforementioned month and was in service until July 1932.

Opposite below IVATT J5 CLASS 0-6-0 NO. 1138
Another Kitson-built J5 was no. 1138. The company produced eight class members during May 1900, including no. 1138 and 1136 (seen above). The first five engines from the batch were employed from new in London.

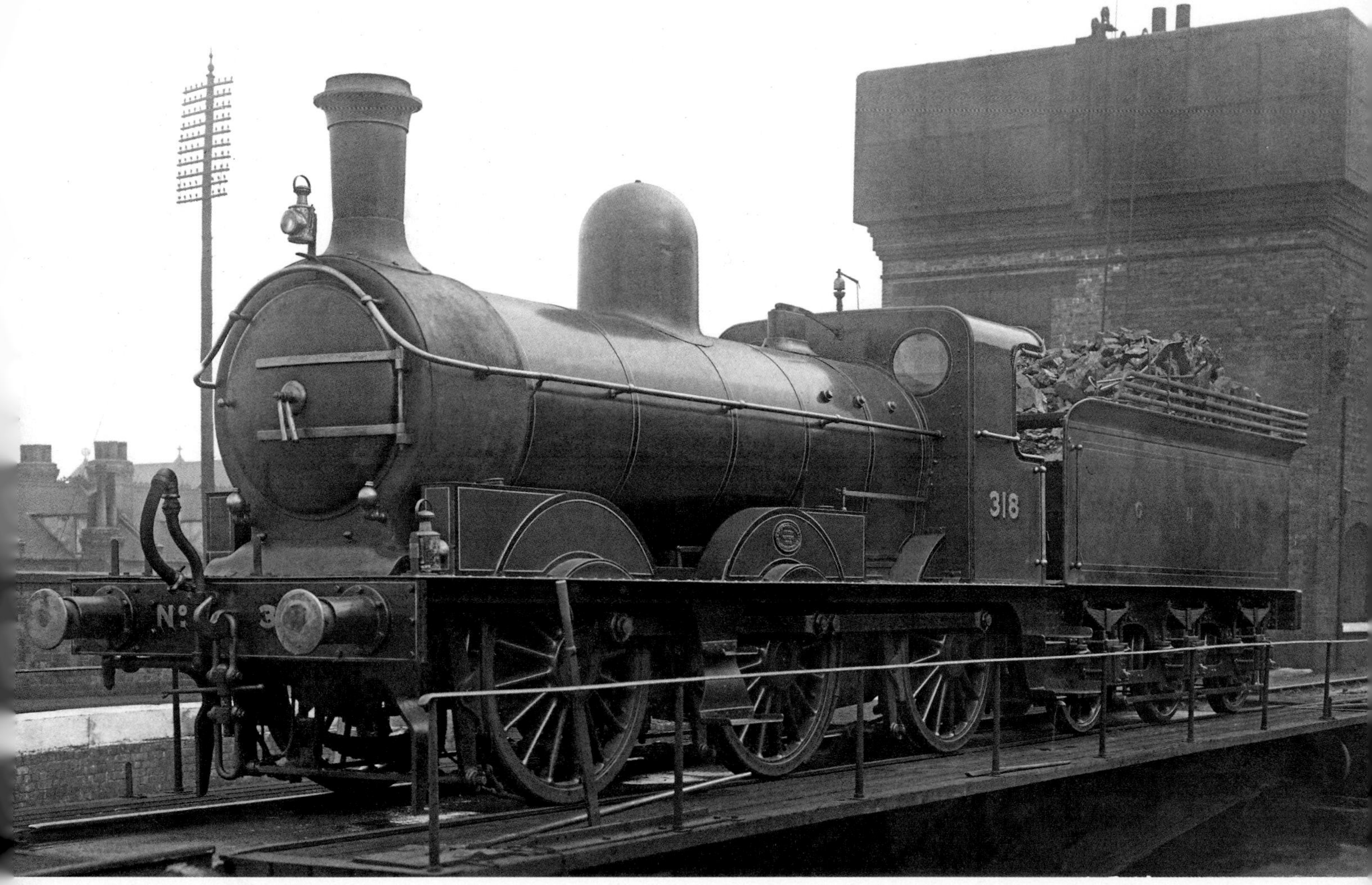
318
Nº 3

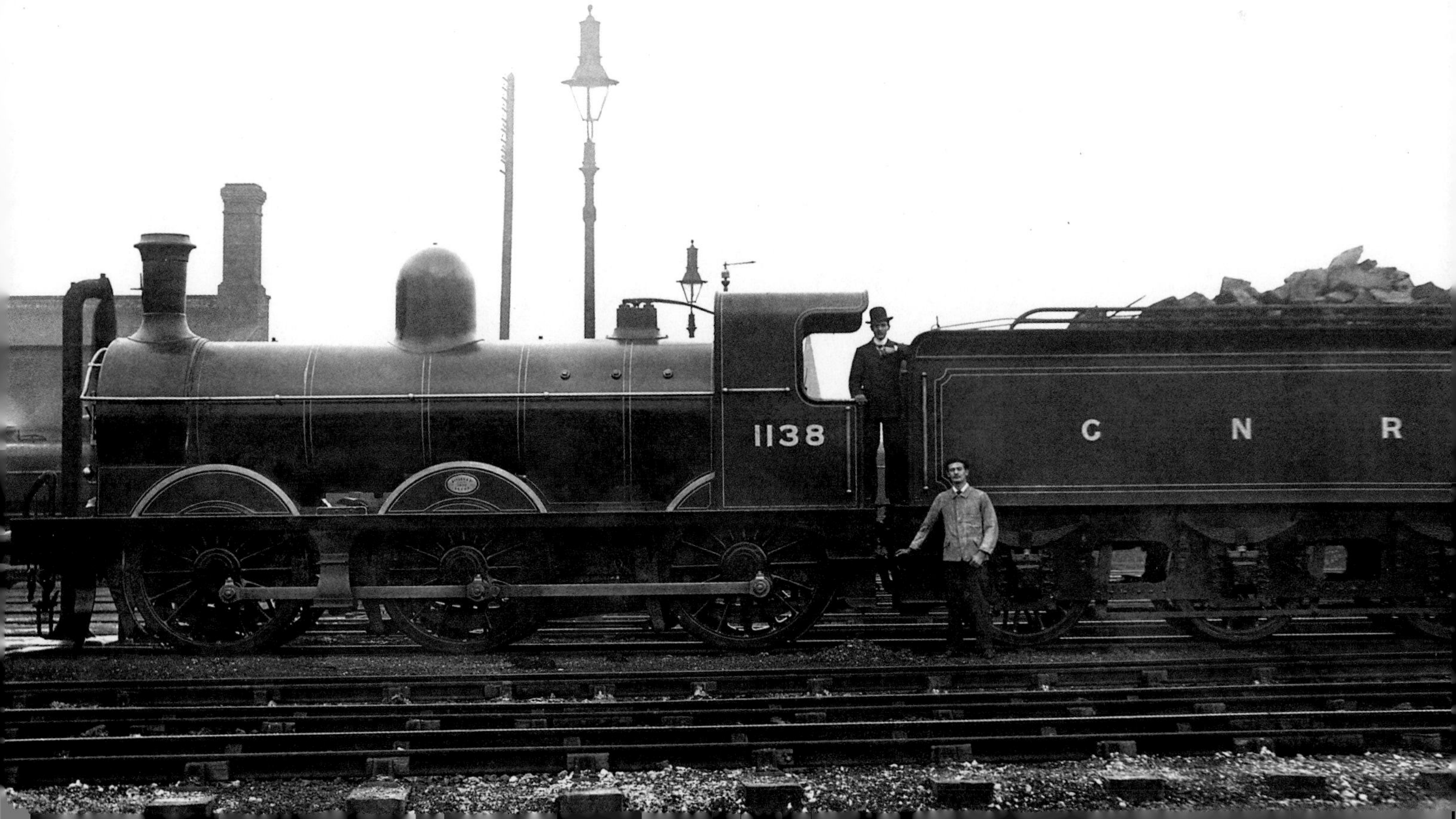
1138
C N R

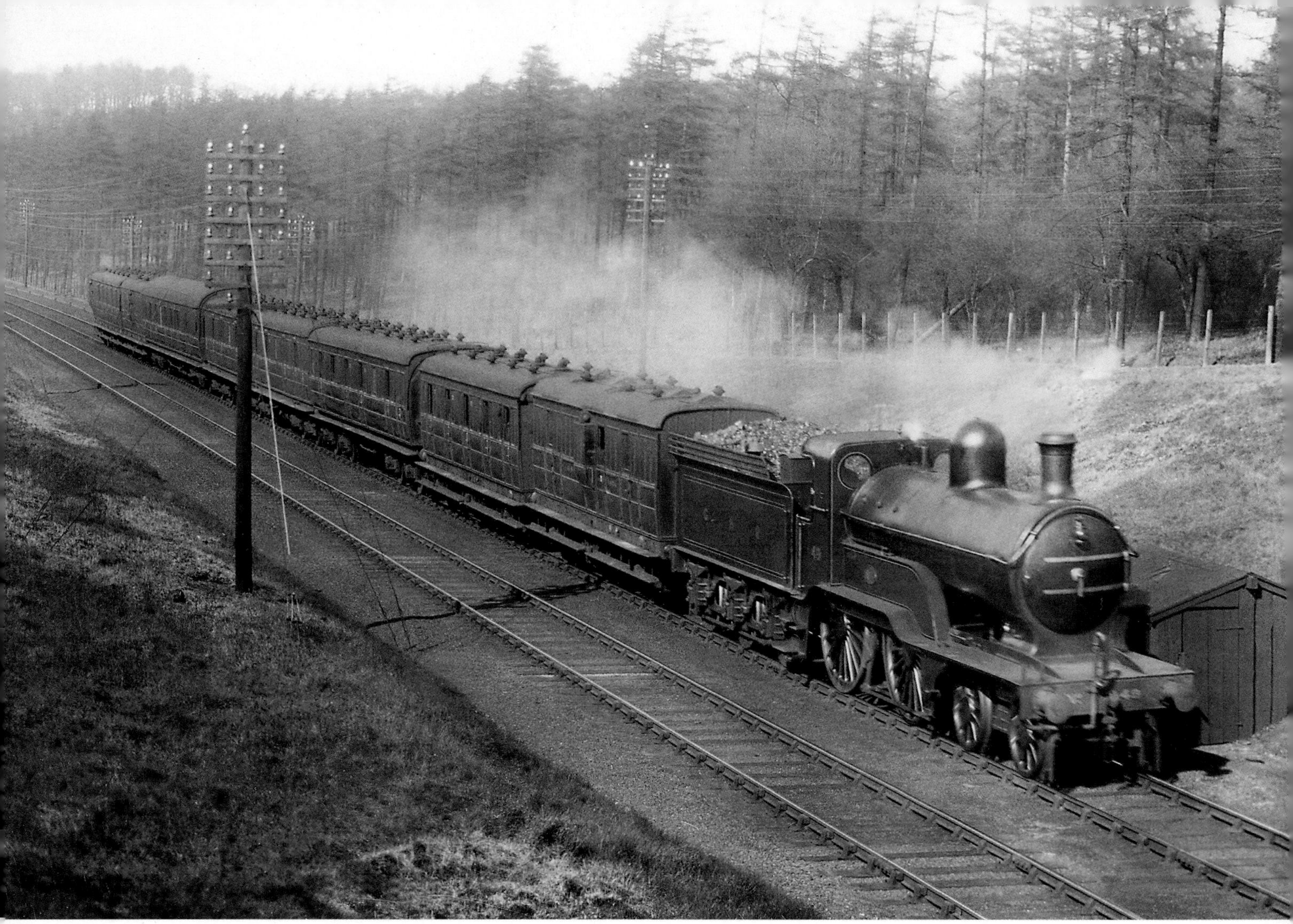

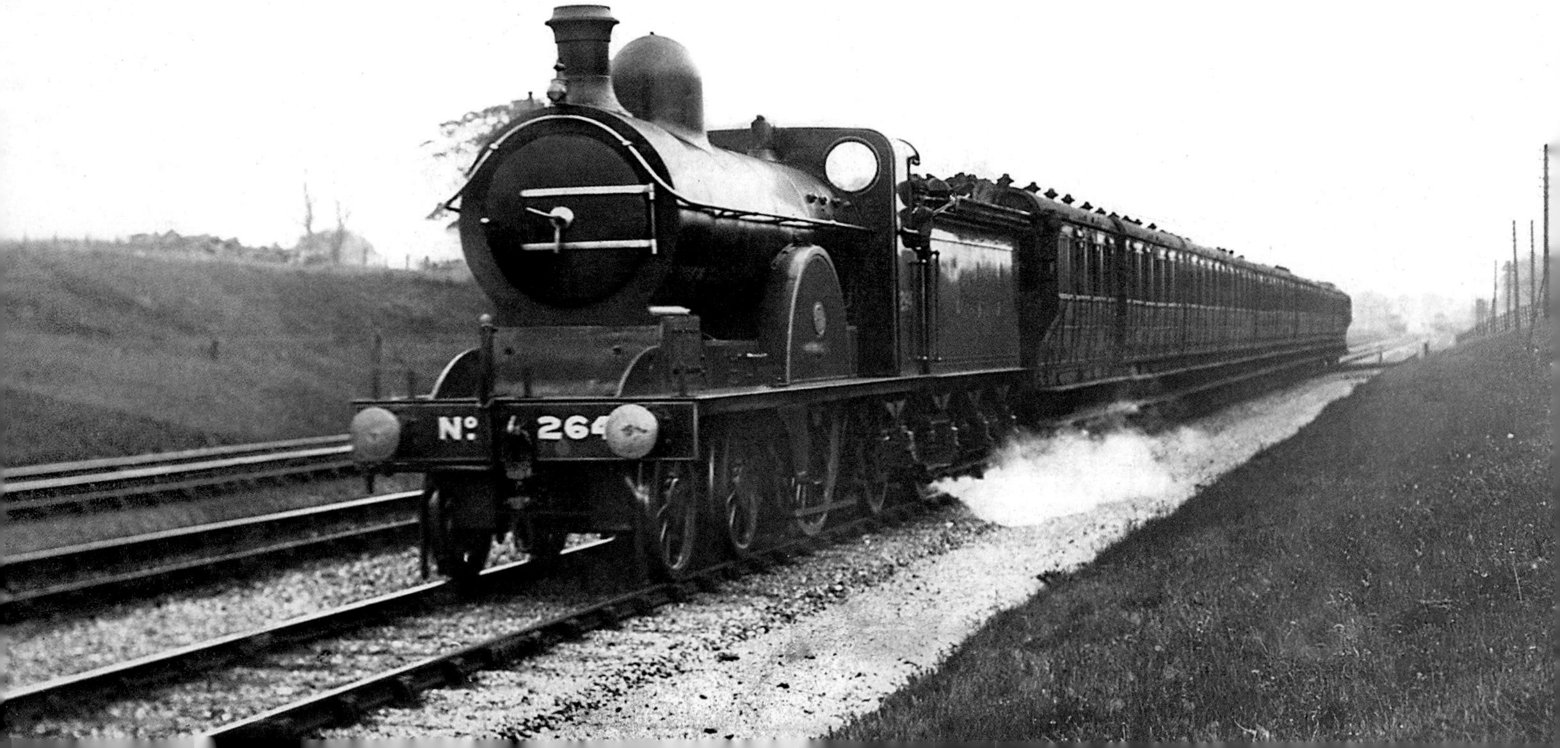
N° 264

Above **IVATT D2 CLASS 4-4-0 NO. 1312**
As a replacement for Stirling's 2-4-0, Ivatt favoured the 4-4-0 wheel arrangement to allow greater stability at the front end. No. 400 was the first GNR 4-4-0 and served as the prototype for the D2 Class which was produced from 1897-1899 when 50 examples were in service. These had Ivatt 4 ft 5 in. diameter boilers with domes, though some had Stirling's brass safety valve covers, and extended cabs. No. 1312 emerged from Doncaster Works in March 1898 and was new to the London area. The engine is pictured here, likely at Doncaster, around the turn of the century.

Opposite above **IVATT D1 CLASS 4-4-0 NO. 49**
With a number of 4-4-0s in service, Ivatt decided to modify the design to extend the availability of the type to more demanding services. The D1 Class had a larger boiler and increased firebox grate area. In 1898, five locomotives were constructed and over the next ten years another 65 entered service. No. 49, which has a passenger train at Ganwick, was amongst the last ten built in 1909, being completed at Doncaster in June and sent to London.

Opposite below **IVATT A5 CLASS 4-2-2 'SINGLE' NO. 264**
Ivatt developed Stirling's 2-2-2 7 ft 6 in. 'Single' to meet the needs of the traffic of the early 20th century. A bogie was provided and a domed 4 ft 5 in. diameter boiler fitted. The first engine had 18¼ in. diameter cylinders and the boiler working at 170 lb per sq. in., whereas the 11 erected subsequently had 19 in. diameter cylinders and the pressure raised slightly to 175 lb per sq. in. No. 264 was built in June 1901 and new to London, though later went to Grantham. All the Ivatt 'Singles' were withdrawn in December 1917.

Below **IVATT D2 CLASS 4-4-0 NO. 1345 – DONCASTER CRIMPSALL REPAIR SHOP**

A dramatic image of D2 Class 4-4-0 no. 1345 being lifted in the Crimpsall Repair Shop at Doncaster Works in the early 20th century. The weight of the engine only, when fully laden, was stated as being 44 tons 7 cwt, with a maximum axle load of 14 tons 9 cwt. When coupled, the tender added a further 38 tons 10 cwt. The water capacity was recorded at 3,170 gallons, though different variants were coupled over the years with higher capacities, the aforementioned figure was the later standard. Similarly, the coal space accommodated 6 tons latterly, but the figure had previously varied. No. 1345 was built at Doncaster in December 1898 and in traffic until just after Nationalisation – withdrawal occurred in January 1949.

Above IVATT D1 CLASS 4-4-0 NO. 1382

An express of 12- and 8-wheel clerestory stock is behind Ivatt D1 Class no. 1382. The locomotive was new from Doncaster in November 1900 and later worked from Peterborough shed. Shortly before Grouping, this had changed to Boston. No. 1382 was one of the early class withdrawals in May 1937. This process began just over six months earlier, yet the last survived to June 1951, undoubtedly due to the Second World War. At Peterborough, the D1s were mainly used on passenger trains between there and King's Cross, though during the First World War the class provided assistance on freight trains. From Boston, the D1s worked to the Lincolnshire Coast, as well as Doncaster, Grantham and Peterborough.

Above IVATT C2 CLASS 4-4-2T NO. 1501
At Wakefield Westgate station with a local train is Ivatt C2 no. 1501 of 1899.

Below IVATT C2 CLASS 4-4-2T NO. 1504
The GNR built a branch line from Alexandra Palace to Enfield in the early 1870s and this was later extended to Stevenage as a diversion from the main line. C2 no. 1504 has a local service at Enfield station – later renamed Enfield Chase – in the early 20th century.

RAIL MOTORS

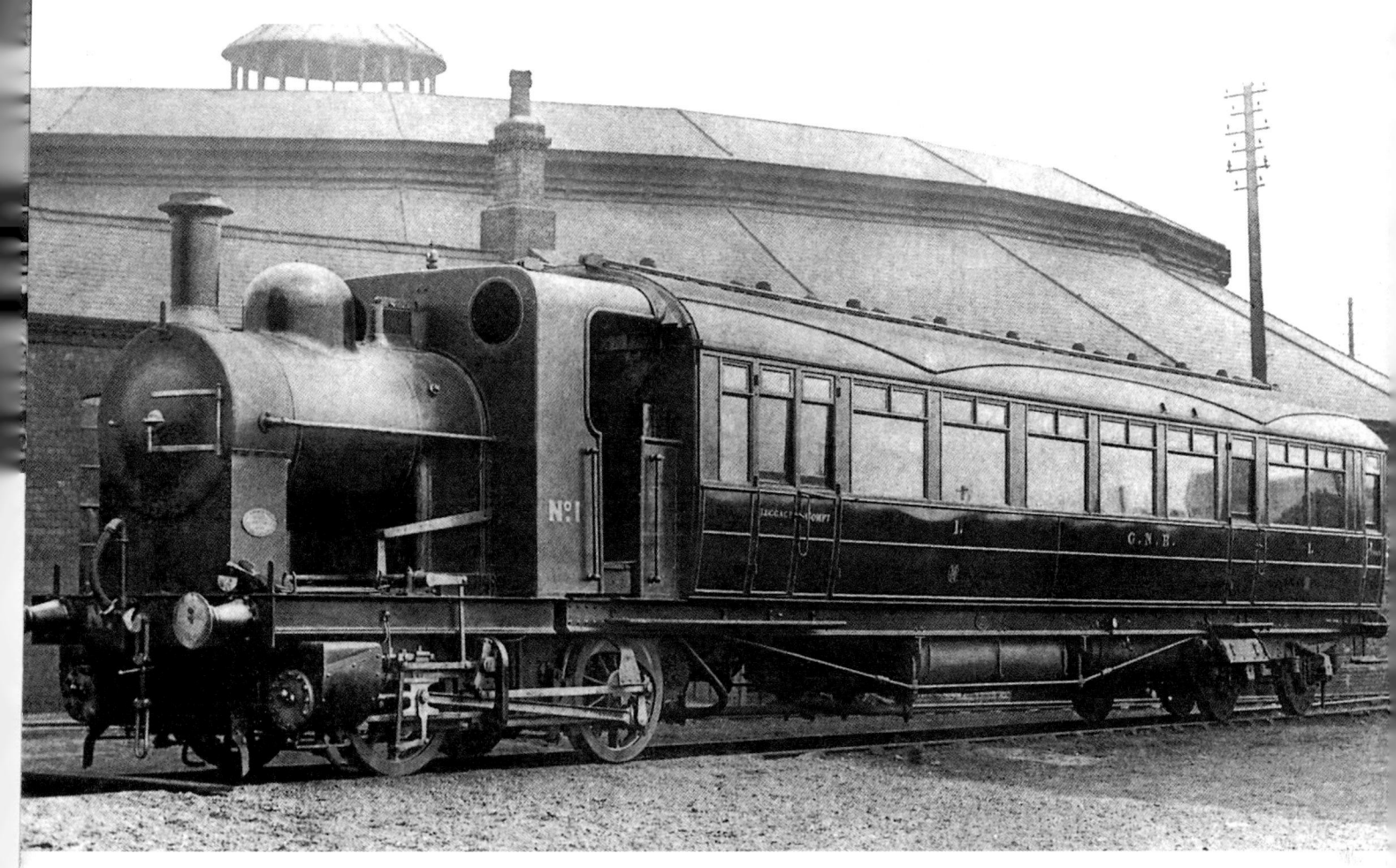

Above IVATT STEAM RAIL MOTOR
Unremunerative branch lines existed long before British Railways and Dr Richard Beeching trimmed many from the national network in the 1950s and 1960s. Often, these had been built by independent companies run by local people interested in improving their daily lives rather than the ability of the route to generate money. With such considerations, the lines often fell into difficulties and led to their takeover by larger companies. These could absorb the costs and take strategic advantage over other railways, making inroads into a particular area by acquiring the route. In an attempt to reduce costs on such lines, many of the pre-Grouping companies sought new methods to serve them, such as petrol railcars and steam-powered carriages. In the early 20th century, the GNR investigated both methods of transporting passengers. Steam rail motors were purchased from the trade, as well as being built at Doncaster Works. No. 1, pictured at King's Cross shed, was one of these and left the shops in late 1905.

Above **IVATT STEAM RAIL MOTOR NO. 7**
Avonside Engine Co.-built no. 7 is pictured at an unidentified location in the early 20th century. After Grouping, the coach bodies of nos 7 and 8 were removed to form an articulated twin set, whilst the engine was scrapped.

Below **IVATT STEAM RAIL MOTOR NO. 6**
Initially sent to work a Grimsby-Louth service, Kitson & Co. steam rail motor no. 6 left to take the Hitchin-Baldock route in 1907 and held the role for a decade. When briefly reinstated during the 1920s, no. 6 was used between Hitchin-Hertford. Photograph courtesy Rail Photoprints.

GNR WAR WORK AND WOMEN WAR WORKERS

Above **WEST CARRIAGE SHOP, DONCASTER WORKS**
Women War Workers are engaged on several tasks in the West Carriage Shop at Doncaster Works on 18th July 1916.

Above TENDER SHOP, DONCASTER WORKS
On 7th July 1915, 18-in. cartridge cases for guns on the front line in France are stacked outside the Tender Shop at Doncaster Works. Even towards the end of 1914, the British Army was experiencing a shortage of shells and this ultimately led to the fall of the Government in 1915. Under the new regime, David Lloyd George was made Minister of Munitions in the ministry of the same name which saw new factories built, existing workshops pushed into war production and men and women conscripted to work in them. The 18-pounder gun was introduced to the British Army during the early 20th century and went on to number around 10,000 examples. The gun fired shrapnel charges initially, though there were also high explosive rounds later developed, as well as other variations. The ammunition consisted of three parts, with the cartridge housing the propellant, then came either the shrapnel round/high explosive/etc., and topped by the fuse. The cartridge cases were manufactured and finished at the workshops before moved on, mostly to a dedicated munitions depot. To meet the demand for cordite, a new process was developed. From a base production number of 500,000 shells in 1914, this method was able to satisfy the requirements for the completion of 50,000,000 in 1917.

Opposite WHEEL SHOP, DONCASTER WORKS
At the back of the Crimpsall Repair Shop, the Wheel Shop spanned the length of the building and was 60 ft long. Several lathes were in use, as well as a wheel press and many of the tools in the shop were driven by electric motors. Two lines were present to move and store the wheelsets, whilst the mobile crane was used to lift them. The scene was captured in 1919 with a female war worker at the controls. Outside the shop, space was provided for storage of wheelsets.

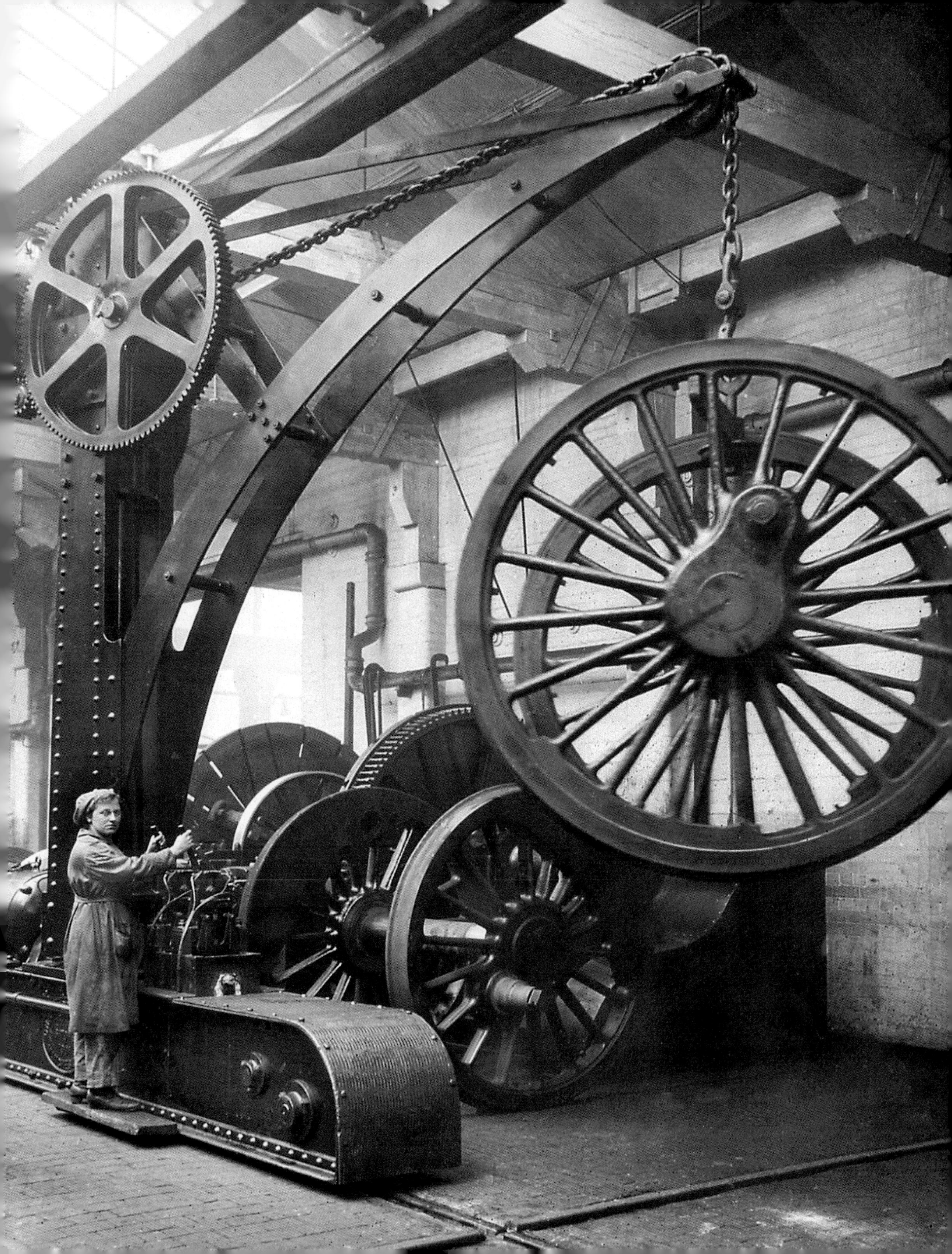

Above **CARRIAGE CLEANERS, DONCASTER WORKS**
An open third-class carriage has the full attention of a group of cleaners at Doncaster Works during July 1916.

Opposite above **TENDER SHOP, DONCASTER WORKS**
Outside the tender shop two stacks of cartridge cases are seen in July 1915. The stack on the right contains approx. 1,270, whilst that on the left has around another 1,280 and that next along the wall even more. For reference, at the start of the Battle of the Somme in 1916, the Royal Artillery sent 1,600,000 shells into enemy positions.

Opposite below **TENDER SHOP, DONCASTER WORKS**
A view taken inside the Tender Shop during 1915. Many more cartridge cases are seen and, on the right, there are two workstations for manufacturing processes to be carried out. In the foreground, metal forms are present for the cases to be slipped over whilst in the background there are small lathes for turning.

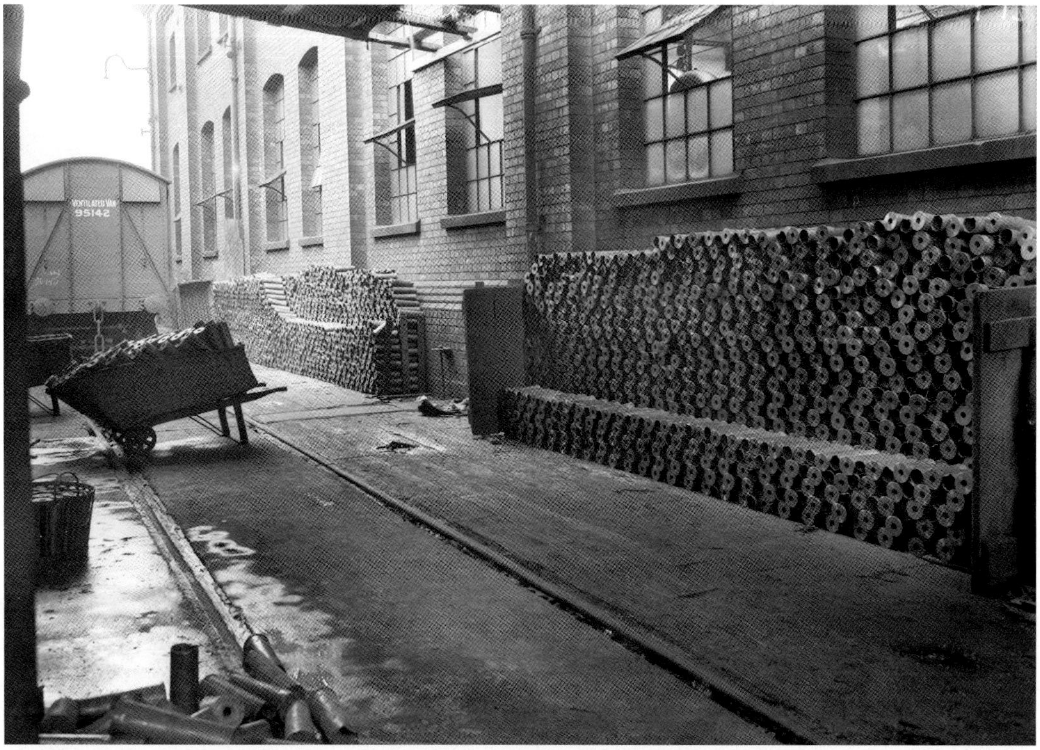

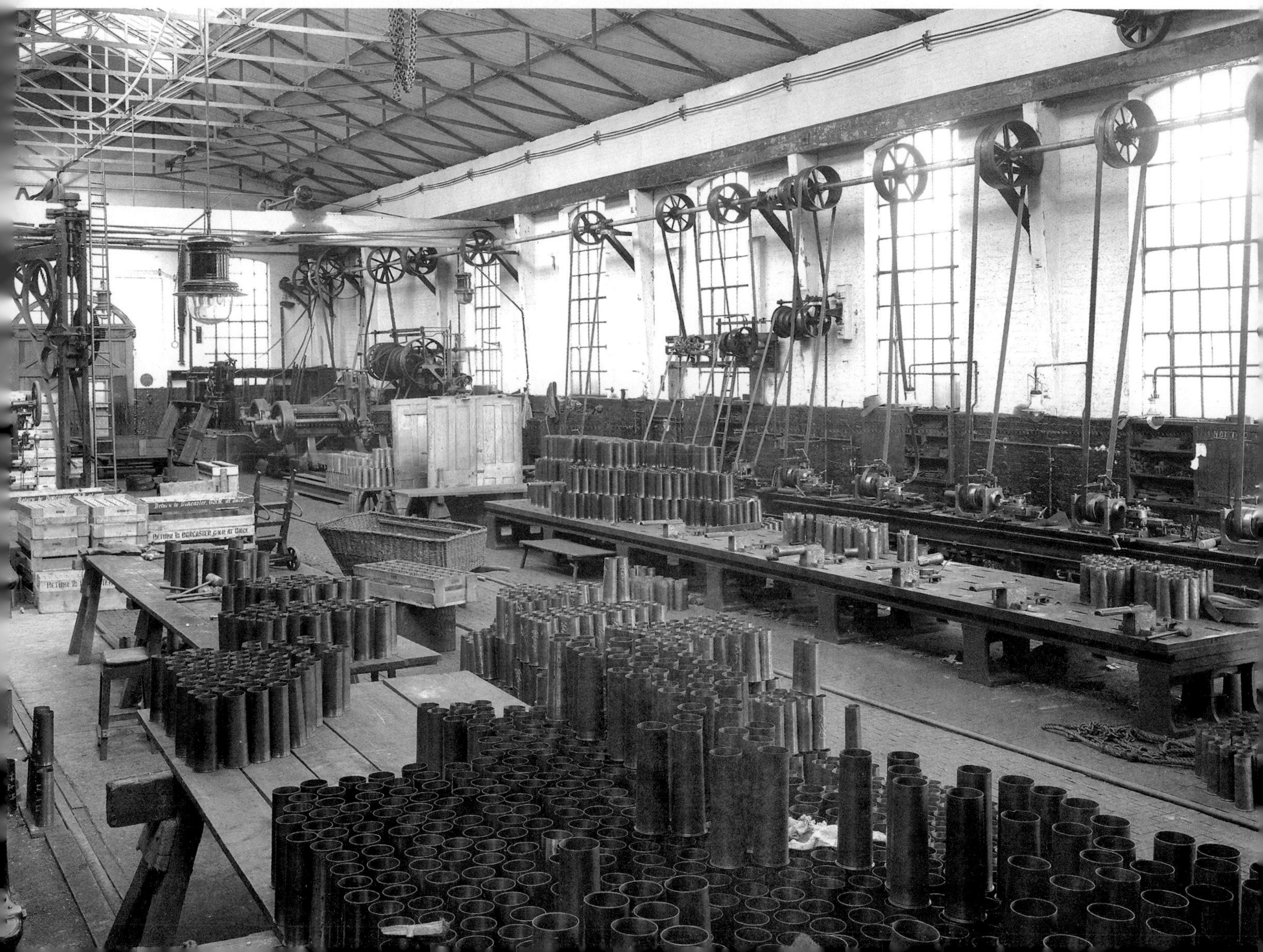

Above **NEW MACHINE SHOP, DONCASTER WORKS**
Male and female workers are engaged on war work in the New Machine Shop during June 1916. Photograph from the David P. Williams Colour Archive.

Opposite above **UPPER TURNERY, DONCASTER WORKS**
This scene was captured in the Upper Turnery in July 1916. A woman war worker is on the left, a youth is facing the camera and in the background between the two is a young boy around ten years of age.

Opposite below **CARRIAGE SHOP, DONCASTER WORKS**
Wagon bodies and chassis are in the course of construction in the Carriage Shop at Doncaster Works. These were to be used for the transportation of war materials, men and casualties.

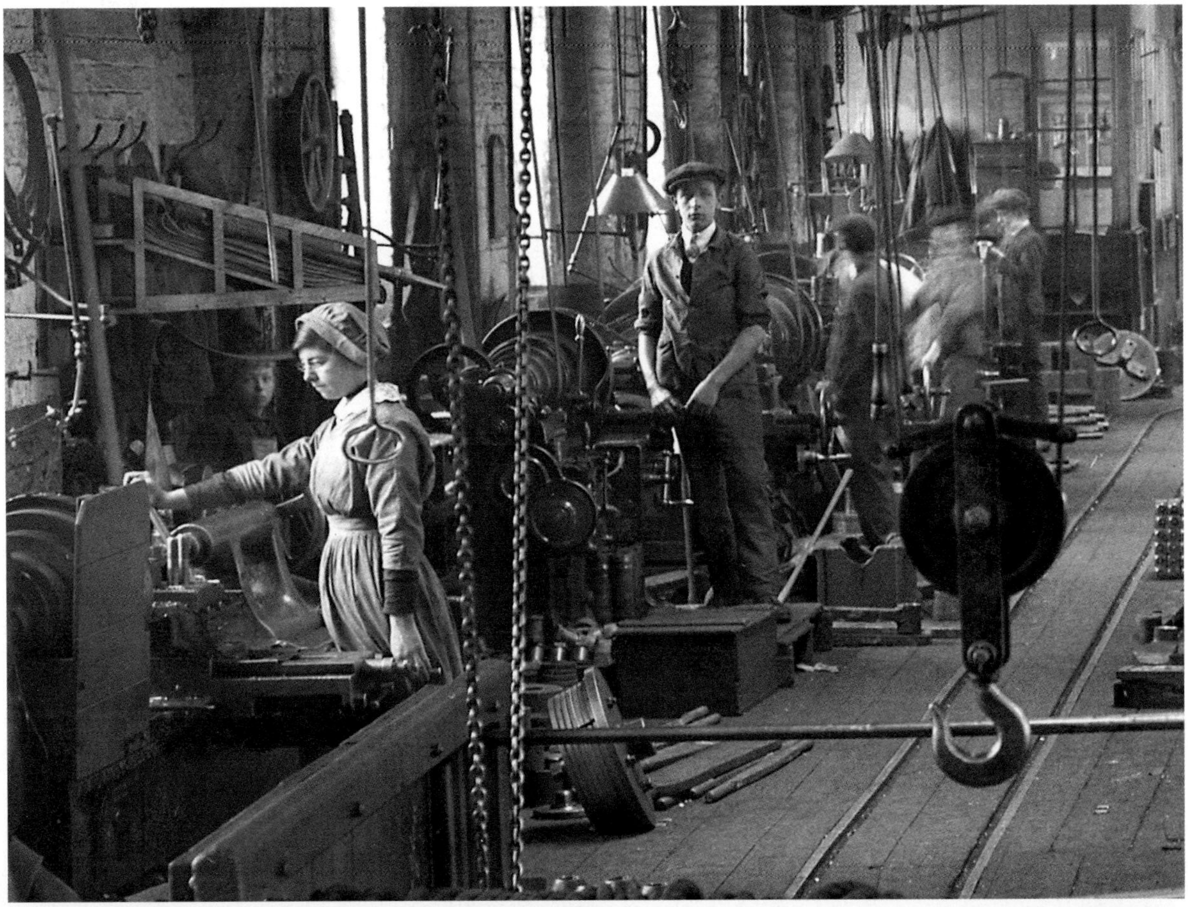

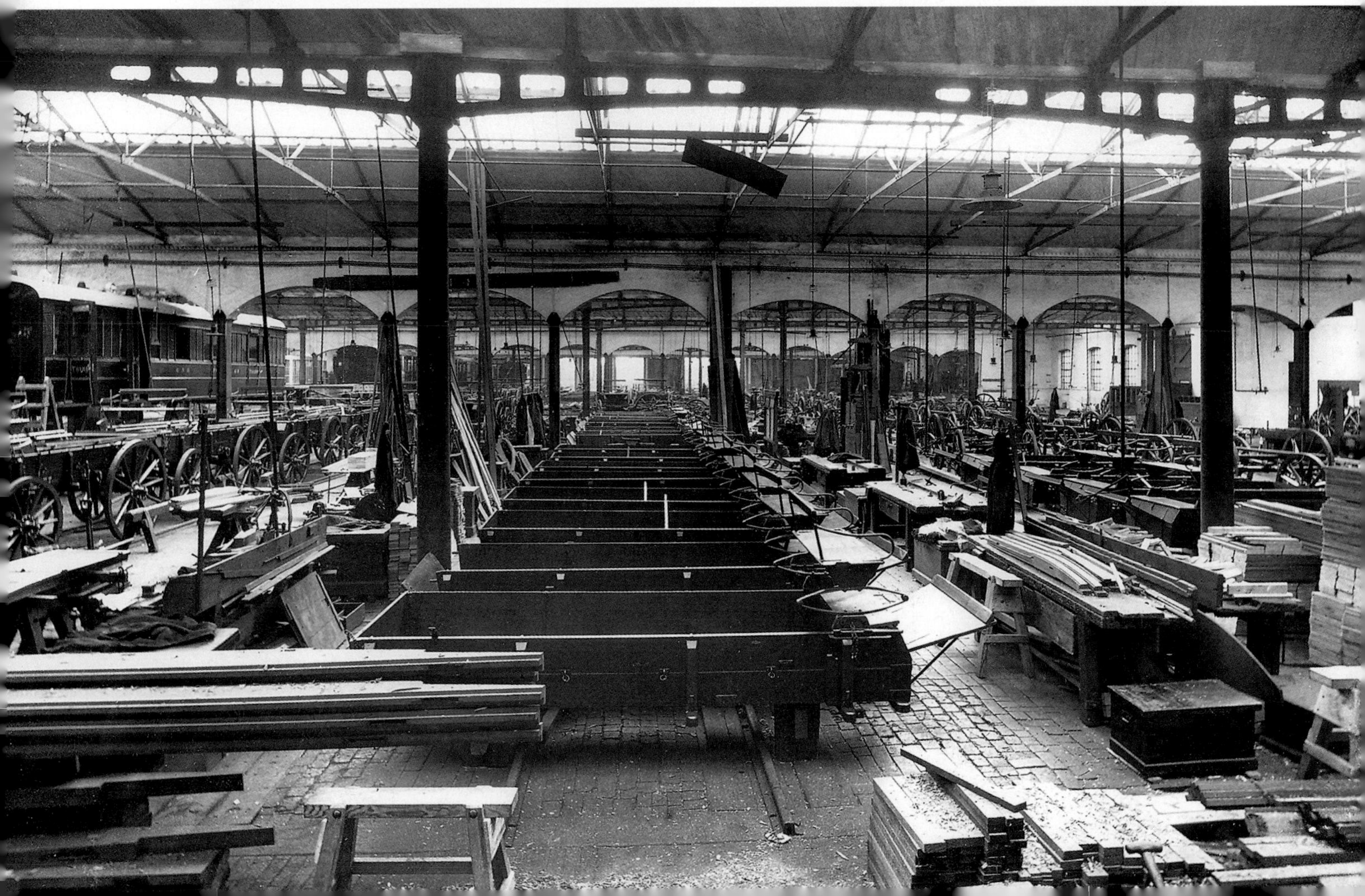

Opposite **NORTH CARRIAGE SHED, DONCASTER WORKS**

Composite carriage no. 1299 has the exterior cleaned in the North Carriage Shed at Doncaster Works during 1916. Five compartments were provided, with two first class (seating 12) and three third class (accommodating 30) in the body which was coupled to a six-wheel chassis.

Below **CARRIAGE CLEANERS, DONCASTER WORKS**

Brake third 12-wheel carriage no. 324 belonged to diagram 54 and was built at Doncaster Works in 1902. The coach was used as part of East Coast Joint Stock operated by all three East Coast companies: GNR, NER and NBR. No. 324 is in the yard near the West Carriage Shop under the attention of carriage cleaners in 1916.

THE GLORIOUS YEARS OF THE GNR – GNR WAR WORK AND WOMEN WAR WORKERS   115

Above and below **PRINCE OF WALES SALOON**
The GNR did not carry much favour with the Prince of Wales, later King Edward VII. In 1875 – reports John Wrottesley in *The Great Northern Railway Volume II* – the Prince was heard to remark "Here's that stuffy old tub again," before boarding the coach and he later had to remove his dog owing to poor air circulation. In 1876, a new saloon was built for the Prince to the design of Patrick Stirling. This was no. 1691 seen here in exterior and interior views. Another carriage was constructed in the late 1880s, though this proved unsuitable and another was not provided until after Edward VII's Coronation.

Above and below **TRAVELLING POST OFFICE**
The first transportation of mail by rail occurred on 11th November 1830 on the Manchester & Liverpool Railway. Companies were later obliged by an Act of Parliament – Railways (Conveyance of Mails) Act 1838 – to transport the post as part of an ordinary or special train. In the same year, the Grand Junction Railway built the first travelling post office by converting a horse box. The GNR's first mail vans appeared around 1849 and by the last quarter of the 19th century five were operational. Travelling Post Office no. 2181 is pictured here c. 1900 and was built at Doncaster in 1885, being 34 ft 1½ in. long and 7 ft 9 in. wide. A corridor connection was provided at one end.

SMOKING
THIRD
THIRD
G N R
THIRD
85
THIRD
THIRD

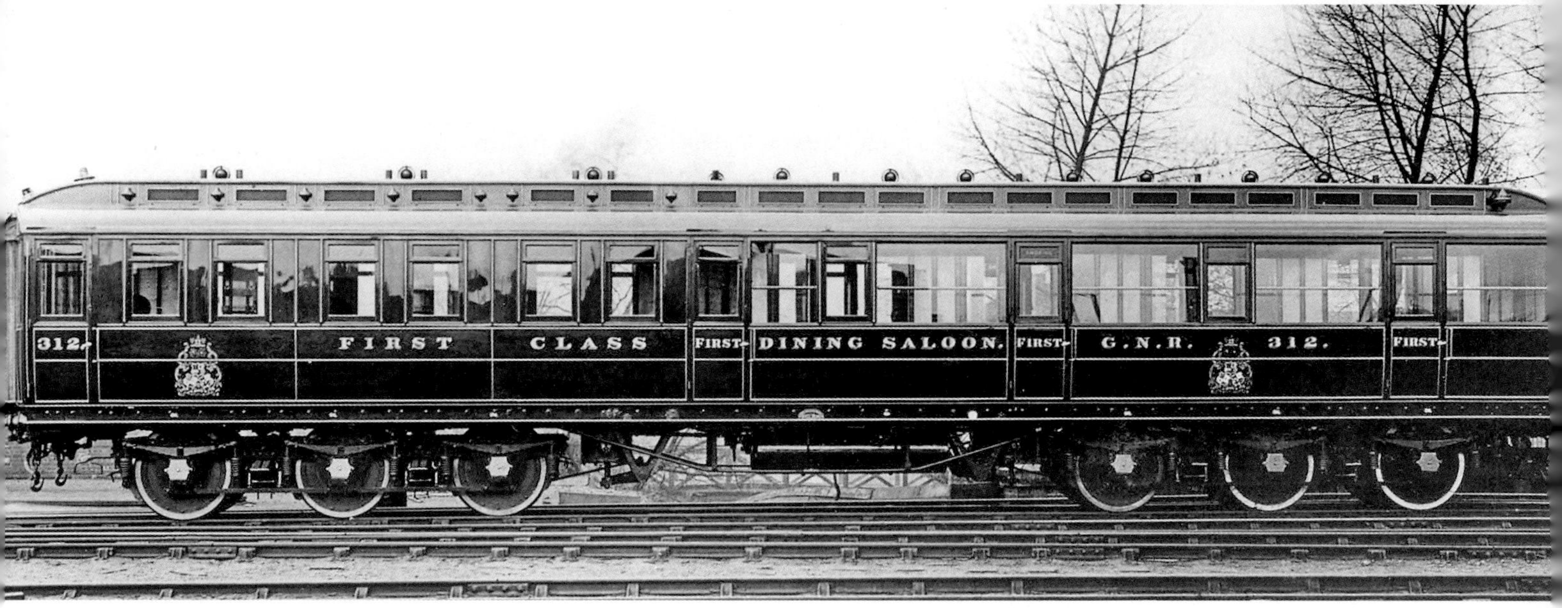
312
FIRST CLASS
FIRST
DINING SALOON.
FIRST
G. N. R.
312.
FIRST

FIRST
G. N. R.
FIRST
2548.
FIRST
THIRD
G. N. R.
THIRD
2548.
THIRD

Above **THIRD-CLASS DINING SALOON NO. 2839**
On the GNR, dining facilities were the preserve of first-class passengers until the mid-1890s when third-class travellers were offered the service. Success had been found earlier in the decade with the ECJS which prompted the GNR to act, first between York and King's Cross, then from the latter to Manchester. No. 2839 was amongst the early examples built and in traffic from Doncaster during 1898. The interior is pictured and shows the three saloons divided to one smoking and two non-smoking sections. The first mentioned had four tables and 12 seats, whilst the other two had six and four tables seating 18 and 12 respectively.

Opposite above **THIRD-CLASS CARRIAGE NO. 85**
John Coffin was the GNR's first Carriage Superintendent, though his tenure only lasted a short time as his death occurred in the late 1850s. John Griffiths took over to the mid-1870s and during this time oversaw the introduction of the East Coast Joint Stock, as well as GNR four-wheel and six-wheel vehicles. He also built one of the first Pullman-style coaches with four-wheel bogie in the early 1870s. E.F. Howlden was appointed in 1876 and held the position for 30 years when succeeded by H.N. Gresley. Howlden was responsible for the construction of around 400 six-wheel third-class coaches over this period, including no. 85, which is seen here at Doncaster in 1910. The carriage was erected in 1890 and provided five compartments for the seating of ten people. Howlden pioneered the use of the corridor coach in Britain.

Opposite middle **FIRST-CLASS DINING SALOON NO. 312**
This 12-wheel dining saloon, no. 312, was pictured in 1900. At one end of the coach, two dining saloons were provided, seating eight and four, whilst four compartments followed and these were flanked by two lavatories.

Opposite below **COMPOSITE CARRIAGE NO. 2548**
Seven diagram 248H composite carriages were built at Doncaster in 1905/1906. No. 2548 was amongst this number and a feature of these was an open seating arrangement for third class, with two areas taking 15 and 18, whilst first class had three compartments taking four people each.

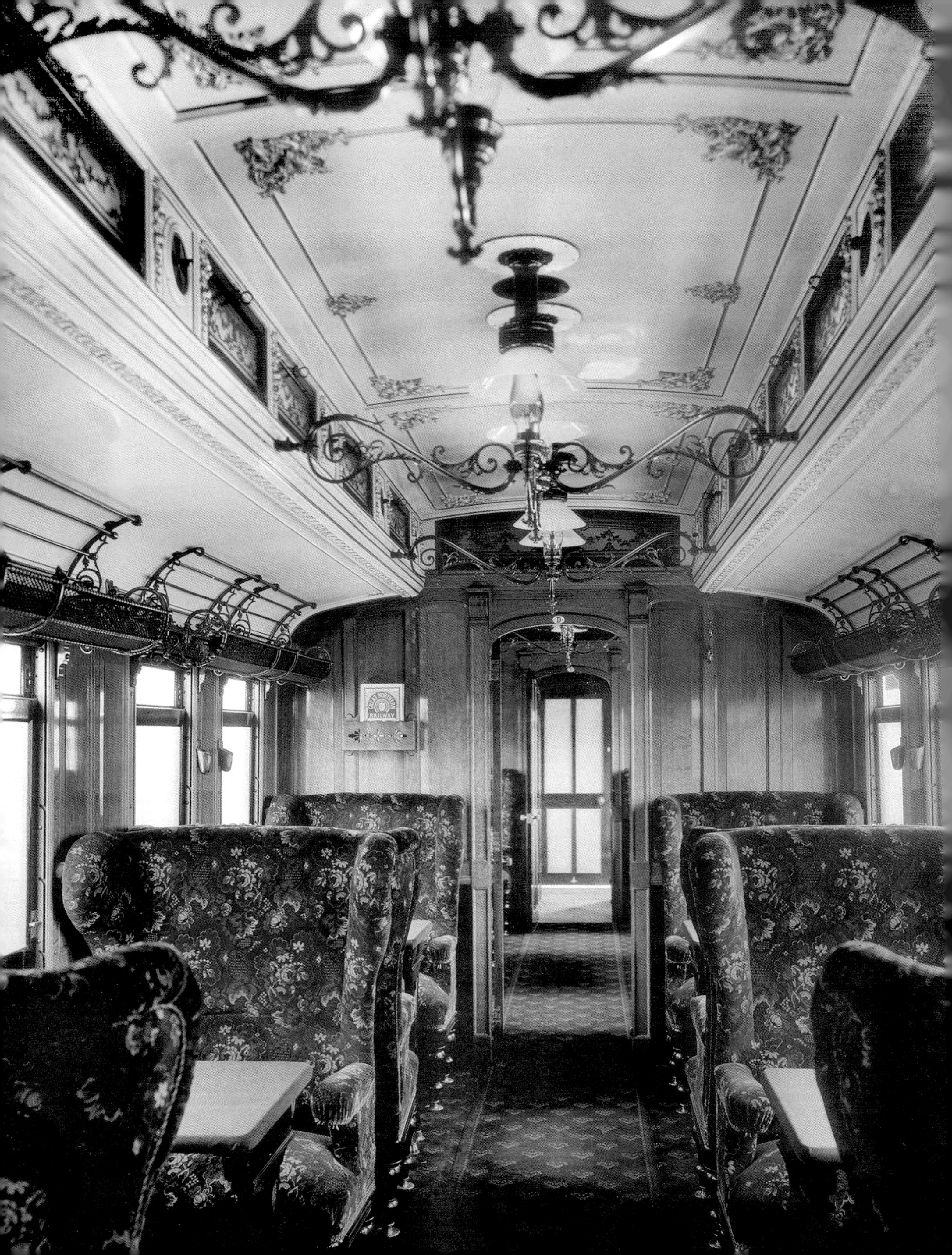

Above **FIRST-CLASS CARRIAGE NO. 208**
On 22nd April 1902, no. 208 was recently completed at Doncaster for use on suburban services. At 28 ft 3 in. long, the carriage was split into four compartments seating first-class passengers. Over 20 were built as part of the order to diagram 409. Photograph from the David P. Williams Colour Archive.

Opposite **FIRST-CLASS DINING SALOON NO. 2836**
The interior of first-class dining saloon no. 2836 is presented here at the end of the 19th century. New at the time, 18 seats were present for passengers as well as a kitchen, pantry, saloon and toilet. Three were built to diagram 52. No. 2836 was later rebuilt as a third-class diner in 1929 and survived to just before the Second World War.

2993 THIRD CLASS DINING SALOON. KITCHEN G.N.R. 2993. FIRST CLASS DINING SALOON. 2993

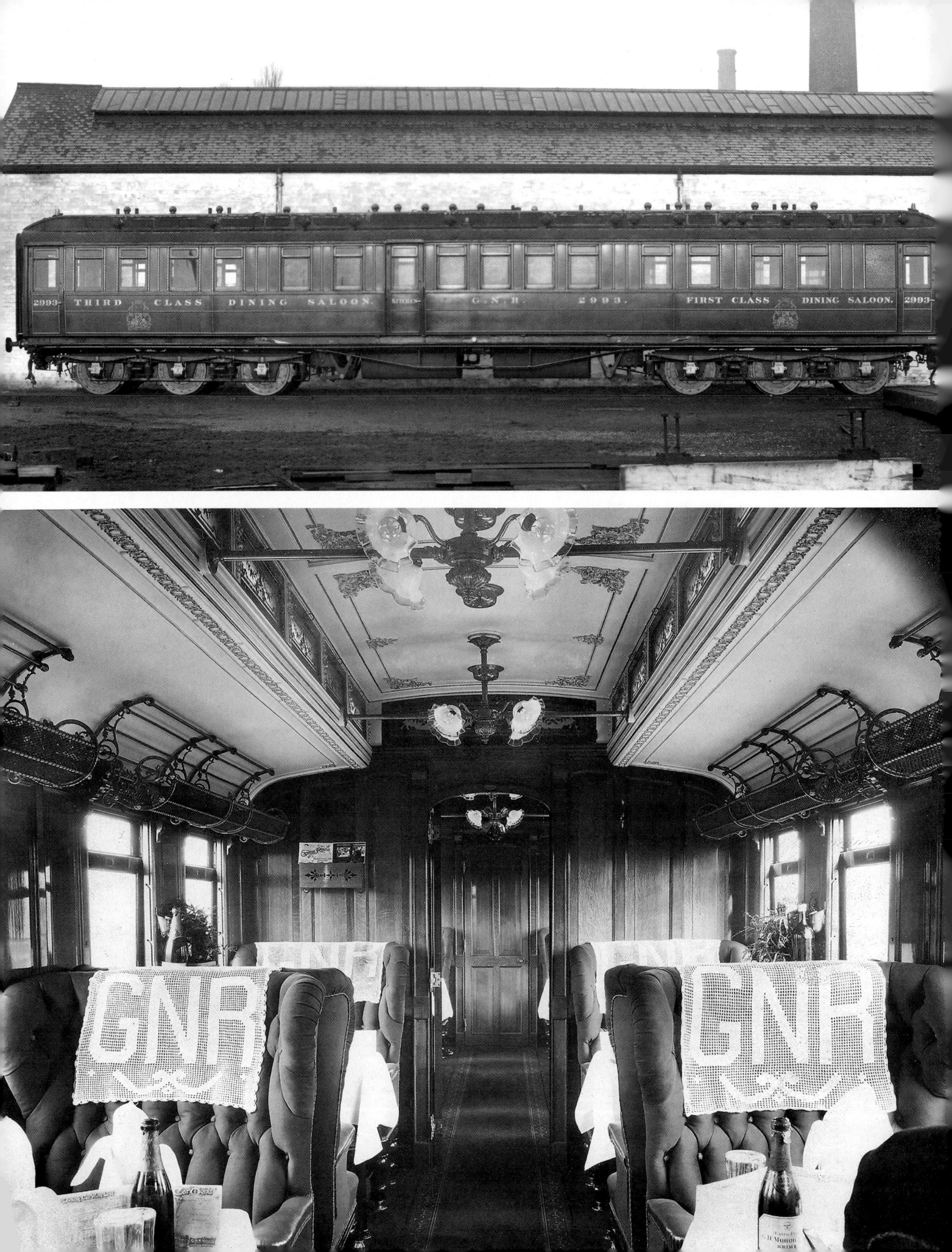

Above **CARRIAGE WORKS STAFF**
Some of the men and boys employed in the Carriage Department at Doncaster Works pose for this image, c. 1910.

Opposite above **COMPOSITE DINING SALOON NO. 2993**
Many railways began using four-wheel carriages before upgrading to six in the late 19th century when more space and greater speeds were deemed desirable. British railways maintained a rigid wheelbase longer than technology demanded owing to the nature of the routes, which had an absence of tight curves where a bogie would have been a necessity. Britain's first bogie carriage was built by the Midland Railway in 1874 and the GNR was quick to join in during the following year. Whilst offering better manoeuvrability, bogies also allowed greater riding stability as well as longer and heavier bodies. In turn, this led to dining facilities, sleeping compartments and lavatories being provided for passengers. Six-wheel bogies were adopted initially as permitted axle loads were quite strict, yet by the turn of the century these were relaxed and allowed many railway companies to change over to four-wheel bogies. The GNR did not do this until H.N. Gresley became Carriage Superintendent in 1905 and 12-wheel composite dining saloon no. 2993 was amongst the later vehicles of the type when pictured during 1904.

Opposite below **FIRST-CLASS DINING SALOON NO. 2581**
No. 2581 was built at Doncaster Works in 1904 and amongst the final contributions to GNR carriage stock by E.F. Howlden. The interior of the coach is depicted opposite and consisted of a smoking saloon seating eight, a non-smoking section for ten followed by a vestibule, pantry and kitchen – there were two other vestibules at either end. The total length of the body was 62 ft and carried by two six-wheel bogies. The ornate decoration applied to the clerestory roof is visible and the lighting was electric.

Below **ROYAL SALOON NO. 395**

Whilst other main line railway companies had suitable facilities for Royal travellers, the GNR, as mentioned, had failed to meet the approval of the Prince of Wales, later King Edward VII. Following an embarrassing incident where the Great North of Scotland Railway's Royal set had to be used in Yorkshire, the GNR and North Eastern Railway resolved to build two carriages for the King and Queen at their respective works. Doncaster produced the King's saloon, no. 395, in 1908 and the day room is below.

Above **ROYAL TRAIN**

In addition to the Royal saloon, several other vehicles were provided as support. They are seen here forming the Royal Train in 1908, though minus the NER's Queen's saloon. The train consists of brake no. 132, saloon no. 1280, saloon no. 3099, King's saloon, saloon no. 3100, brake no. 32. Ivatt 'Atlantic' no. 1448 plays the role of the 'Royal engine'.

Below **COMPOSITE DINING SALOON NO. 3039**

One of Gresley's first tasks as Carriage & Wagon Superintendent was to produce new coaches for the King's Cross to Sheffield and Manchester service. Composite dining saloon no. 3039 was amongst this so-called 'Sheffield stock' when built in 1906 and is seen close to completion – the two six-wheel bogies are yet to be fitted – at Doncaster's carriage shops. Seating was for eight and 18 in first- and third-class respectively.

E.C.J.S.
THIRD
176.

LONDON (KINGS CROSS) AND PERTH VIA FORTH BRIDGE
240.
FIRST
EAST COAST.
THIRD
THIRD
240.
PASSENGERS
LUGGAGE

252
EAST COAST. THIRD CLASS.
252

Above **FIRST-CLASS DINING SALOON NO. 193**
Whilst many of the ECJS carriages were built by the railway companies, a number were also purchased from the trade. No. 193 was one of three saloons obtained from the Lancaster Carriage & Wagon Co. in 1893 for the early afternoon King's Cross-Edinburgh service. Two saloons were provided for first-class passengers – smoking and non-smoking – and seated a total of 24. A feature of the trio was the provision of two four-wheel bogies.

Opposite above **THIRD-CLASS CORRIDOR NO. 176**
At the end of the 1880s, the diagram 20 third-class corridor carriage first entered service. These had five compartments, 6 ft 1 in. wide, seating six each. Two toilets were also provided at either end. Six were built at Doncaster initially, then five appeared in 1890 and finally six entered service in 1891.

Opposite middle **COMPOSITE BRAKE NO. 240**
In the second half of the 1890s, the first ECJS 12-wheelers started work on the ECML. Seven composite brake carriages were built at Doncaster, including no. 240. There were two compartments each for first- and third-class passengers, separated by a toilet, and these accommodated eight and 12 people respectively. The first-class compartments were 7 ft 2 in. wide, whilst the third class were 6 ft 3 in.

Opposite below **OPEN THIRD NO. 252**
Another early 12-wheeler was no. 252. An open third, seating was split into three saloons, two of which were 12 ft 6 in. long and the other was 18 ft 9 in. These had room for 15, 16 and 23 respectively, whilst at one end a pantry was provided, along with attendant's cupboard and toilet. A total of three were built to diagram 28 in 1896.

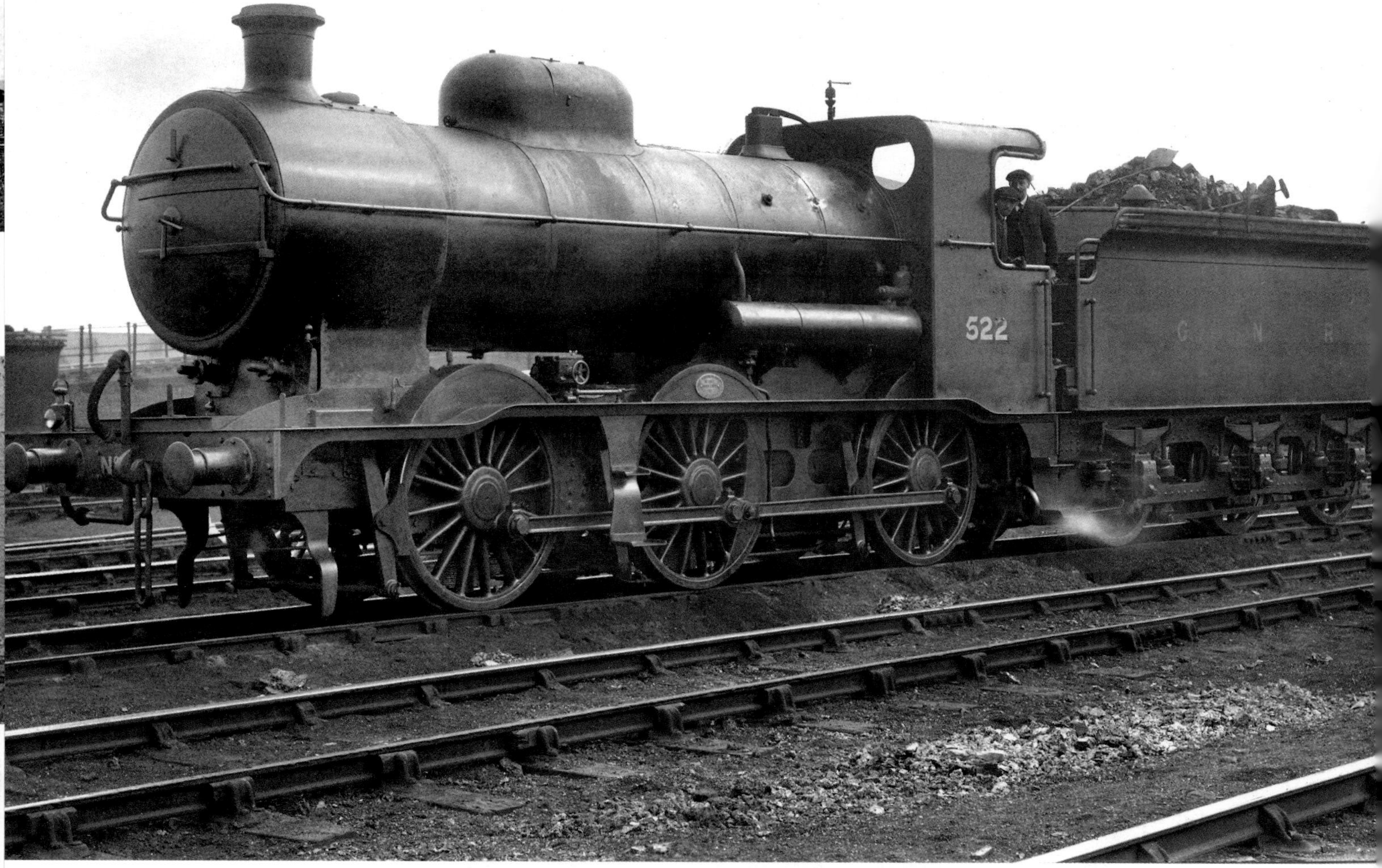
522
G N R

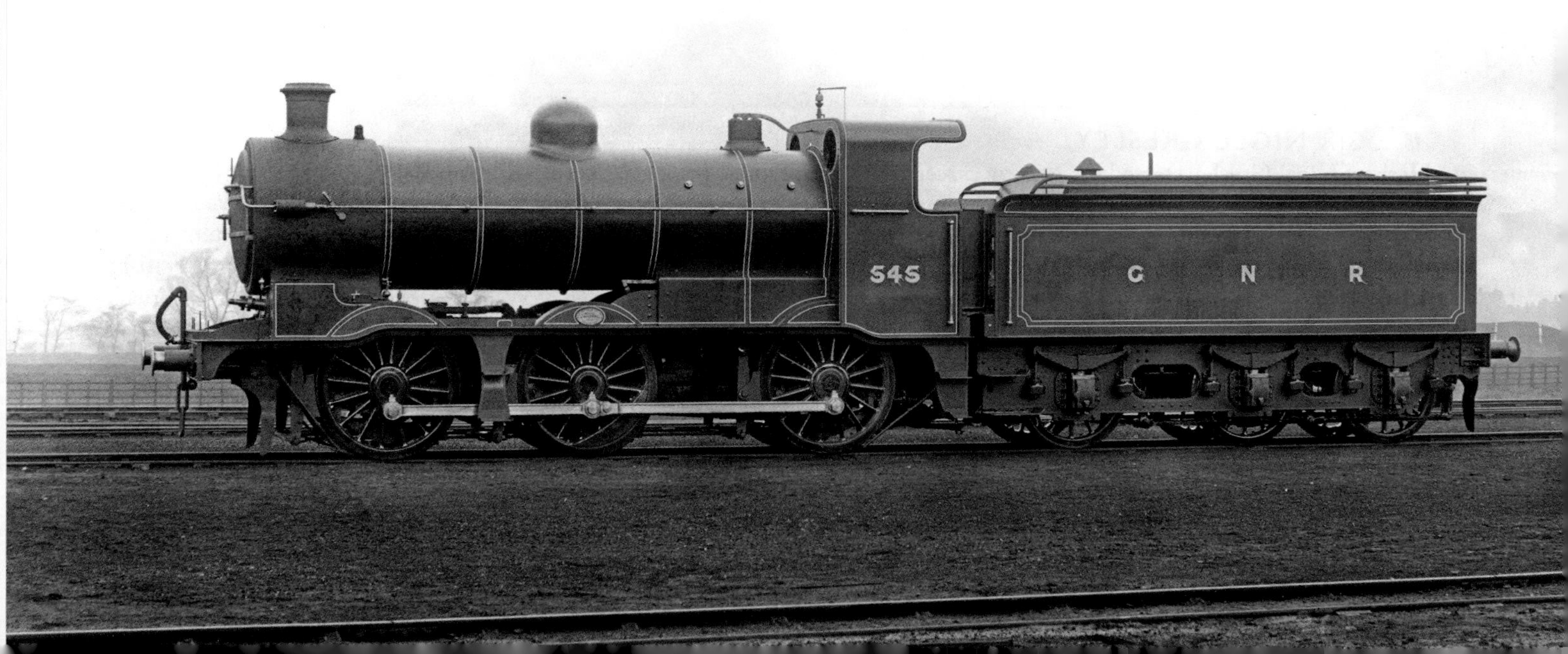
545
G N R

Above **IVATT/GRESLEY J22 CLASS 0-6-0 NO. 546**
No. 546 was the first of 30 J22s built in 1913 and this group had changes in superheater type. The first five had Robinson 18-element superheaters, the next 15 had the original Schmidt-type, whilst six, nos 561-566 had a superheater designed by Doncaster Drawing Office. Five had the 'straight tube' type and one was equipped with Gresley's 'twin tube' superheater. The Schmidt and Robinson arrangements were further perpetuated in subsequent construction, though Gresley ultimately favoured the latter.

Opposite above **IVATT/GRESLEY J22 CLASS 0-6-0 NO. 522**
As Ivatt was leaving office, 15 J22 Class 0-6-0s, which were superheated, appeared from Doncaster Works. These were known as the 521 series and followed up by the 536 series with detail differences implemented by Gresley. No. 522 was the second of the 521 series built in September 1911 and subsequently entered trials with a feedwater heater. In 1916, the locomotive was fitted with a second dome which received water to be slightly heated before entering the boiler. A secondary process also occurred whereby impurities were filtered from the water. In service, this filter was found to be too good and scale formation led to a 'mud collector' – a secondary cylinder mounted at the side of the firebox – to provide additional filtration. No. 522 has both pieces of apparatus here in this image from 1918. The experiment concluded for the engine in 1923.

Opposite below **IVATT/GRESLEY J22 CLASS 0-6-0 NO. 545**
Nearly a year after the 521 series had been completed, the first of Gresley's 536 series appeared from Doncaster. Ten were built at the end of 1912 with no. 545 the last in traffic. The alterations from Ivatt's engines included repositioned boiler and sandboxes, as well as smaller cab. A further 85 locomotives were constructed to similar specifications up to 1922.

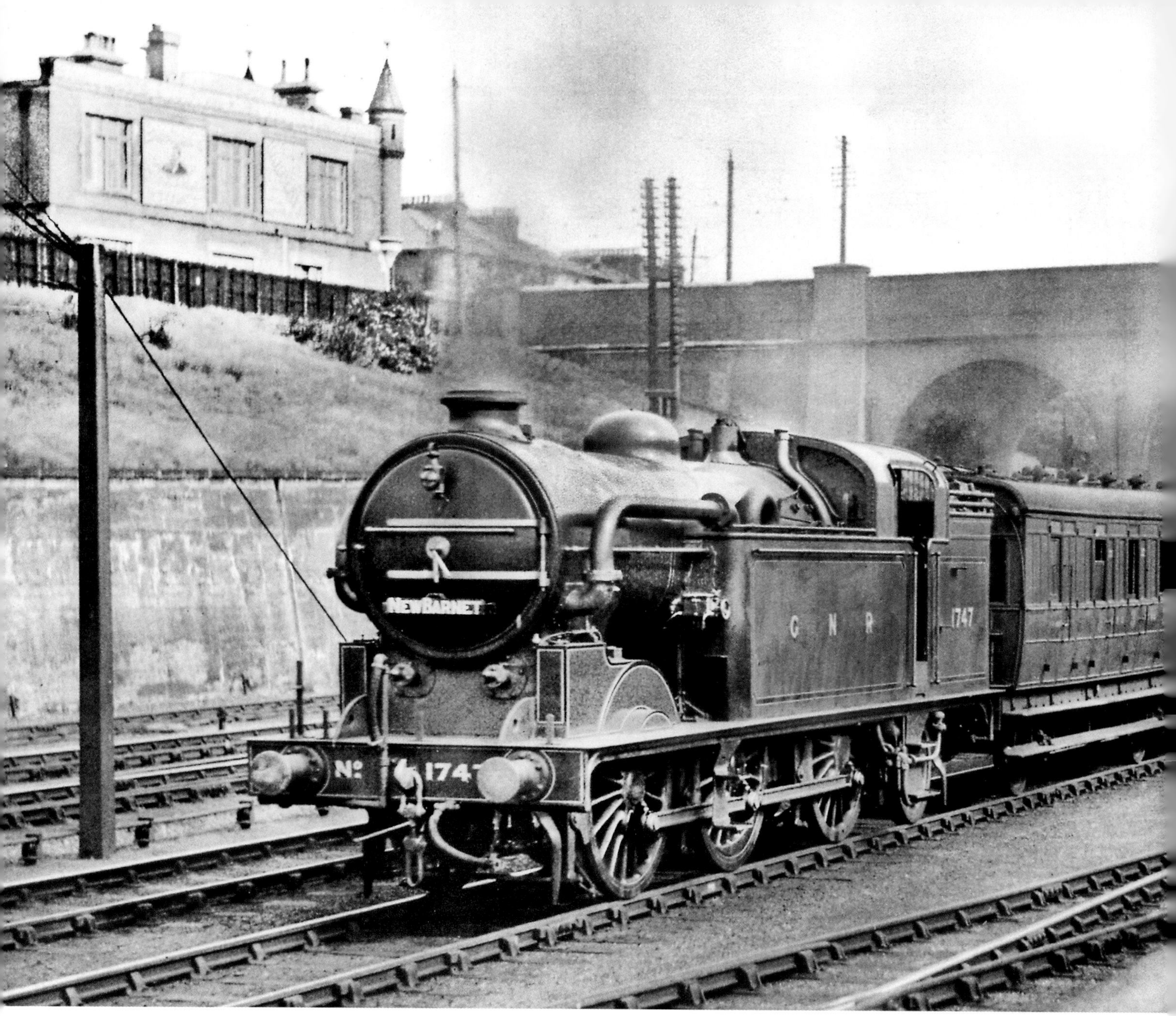
NEW BARNET
No 1747
G N R
1747

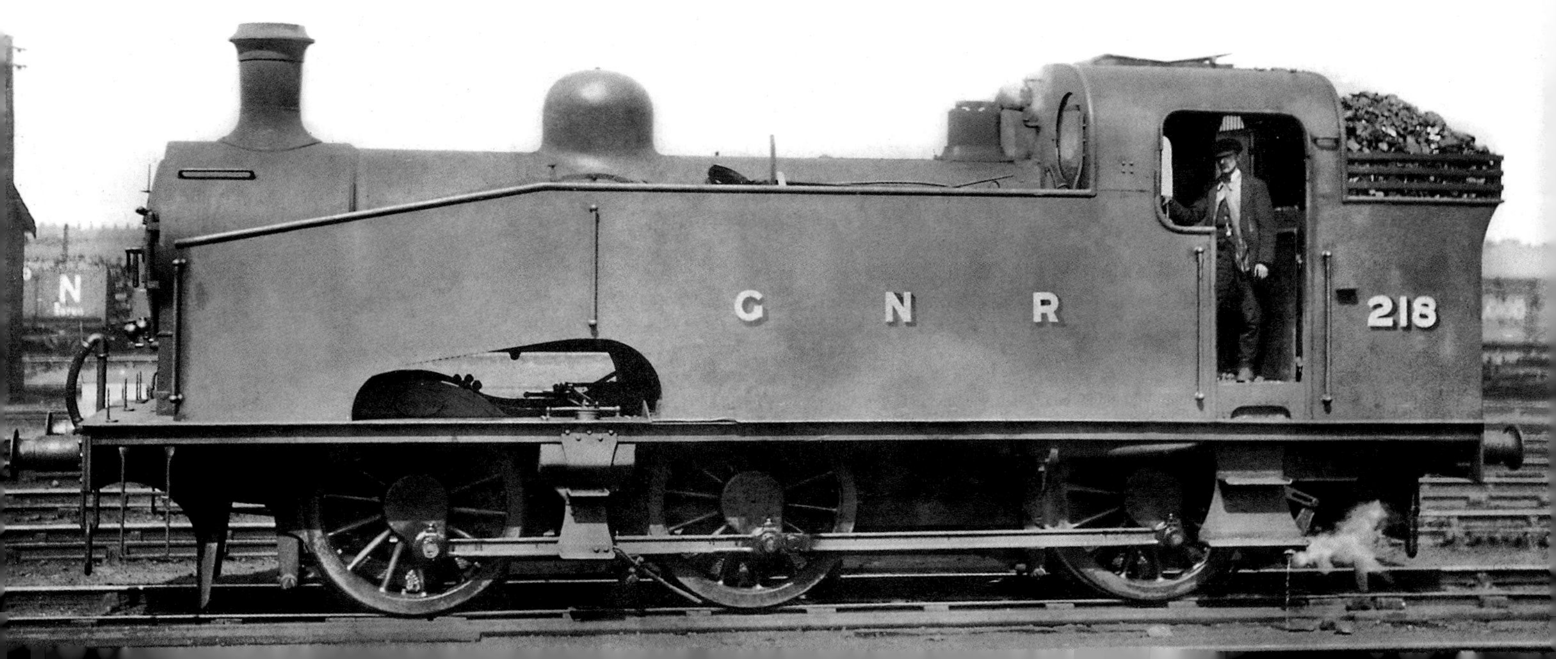
G N R
218

Opposite above **GRESLEY N2 CLASS 0-6-2T NO. 1747**
Ivatt's N1 Class served suburban services well until the late 1910s when improved engines were necessary. Gresley produced the N2 Class which had bigger cylinders, piston valves and a superheated boiler. Sixty were completed in just a short period – 1920-1922 – with ten at Doncaster and 50 from the North British Locomotive Company. No. 1747 was constructed at the latter works in March 1921 and is seen when relatively new with a northbound train leaving New Southgate station.

Opposite below **GRESLEY J23 CLASS 0-6-0T NO. 218**
The first of a new series of shunting engines for employment in the West Riding of Yorkshire appeared from Doncaster in late 1913. A total of 40 were eventually produced in three groups of ten, twenty and ten. No. 218 was amongst 20 forming the 168 series which had improved weight distribution amongst other detail changes. In service during August 1919, no. 218 was new to Ardsley shed where duties included shunting in the local goods yard and transfer freight movements locally.

Below **GRESLEY N2 CLASS 0-6-2T NO. 1742**
Another NBLC N2 is pictured and no. 1742 stands in the yard at King's Cross shed in mid-April 1921. Most of the 60 GNR N2s (more were built by the LNER) worked from King's Cross shed, with a small number at Hatfield and Hornsey, in addition to one at Hitchin. King's Cross kept around 60 N2s employed on suburban trains and empty stock movements to the late 1950s, with no. 1742 surviving there to August 1959.

Above **GRESLEY H4 CLASS 2-6-0 NO. 1003**
The First World War put locomotive developments on hold, yet did not stop Gresley from planning for the end of the conflict. Before introducing his first three-cylinder locomotive in 1918, Gresley proposed a third version of his 2-6-0 with higher boiler pressure to increase the haulage capacity. This was left on the drawing board but following the success of the three-cylinder 2-8-0, a 2-6-0 with a much bigger boiler – 6 ft 0 in. diameter, which was the largest in use at the time – was put in hand at Doncaster in mid-1919. Ten of the H4 Class were built in 1920 and 1921, with no. 1003 in traffic from October 1920. The locomotive is at New Southgate with a northbound train in the following year. N2 Class no. 1726 is also visible on a local train.

Below **GRESLEY H4 CLASS 2-6-0 NO. 1000**
Whilst Gresley's modern engineering practices were being implemented, he neglected to provide adequate shelter for footplatemen for several years. The H4 Class was built with Ivatt cabs, though with extended canopies and slightly larger look-outs. Despite the engine being particularly large, the tender was small in comparison, if adequate for the duties assigned the locomotives. The cab of the first H4, no. 1000, is new here in early 1920. Much of the regulator mechanism was the same as used previously for Doncaster's locomotives, but the regulator handles, on each side of the cab and connected by a rod spanning the top of the firebox, were new in operating by lifting rather than horizontal movement. No. 1000's regulator proved difficult to move and the other nine H4s had the old arrangement.

Above **KNEBWORTH STATION**
Whilst some landowners actively fought railway interests, the Earl of Lytton at Knebworth gave land for sidings in the area and encouraged housing developments around the station when opened in 1884.

Below **KING'S CROSS STATION**
Lewis Cubitt designed King's Cross station and construction took 18 months to opening in mid-October 1852. The frontage facing Euston Road was 216 ft long with central 112-ft-tall clock tower. Several structures subsequently cluttered the entrance though recently these have been removed.

Above **LOFTHOUSE & OUTWOOD STATION**
The men and boys employed at Lofthouse & Outwood station pose for the camera in the early 20th century. Opened in 1858 as Lofthouse, the addition to the title was made in the mid-1860s.

Below **NEW SOUTHGATE STATION**
Several name changes affected New Southgate station, which opened as Colney Hatch on 7th August 1850. Even originally, the name was to be Betstile after an earlier title of the area. In 1855, Southgate dominated over Colney Hatch and Friern Barnet before becoming the sole name in 1971.

Above **PETERBOROUGH STATION**
Branches from the London & Birmingham and Eastern Counties Railways' lines converged in a joint project at Peterborough in the mid-1840s. When the 'Lincolnshire Loop' opened, the GNR used the station, yet soon resolved to create a new facility for the completion of the main line. Peterborough station was ready from 1850 and at Grouping became Peterborough North and the aforementioned was renamed Peterborough East.

Below **POTTERS BAR STATION**
A porter with milk churn, passengers, station staff and signalmen have paused for this image to be taken at Potters Bar, c. 1900. The original station was replaced in the 1950s and this too has since been demolished for a new facility.

Above **RANSKILL STATION**
Despite being in a relatively unpopulated area, Ranskill station was a substantial building in use from 1849 until closed by BR in 1958. From the Second World War, the station's importance improved due to the opening of a Royal Ordnance Factory nearby.

Below **ROSSINGTON STATION**
Seven miles north of Ranskill, Rossington station visibly shares the same architecture. Though later serving a large colliery village, Rossington was also closed in 1958. Whilst Ranskill has been demolished, Rossington survives as a private residence.

Opposite **STANLEY STATION**

The Bradford, Wakefield & Leeds Railway wanted to connect with the wider network in the 1860s. The company promoted a short connection to the Midland Railway and North Eastern Railway west of Castleford. This was the Methley Joint Railway which also had the latter and Lancashire & Yorkshire allowed running powers. Ready for traffic in mid-1865, one of the two stations built was Stanley. Just before the opening of the MJR, the GNR formally absorbed the BW&LR, though the project continued to be a joint venture with the NER and L&YR.

Below **WOOD GREEN STATION**

Wood Green was a small, exclusive area of North London, with inhabitants numbering less than 500 in the mid-1850s. A station opened there in 1859, though soon after, housing developments occurred in Wood Green and the Alexandra Palace was built in the 1860/1870s. Before a branch was completed to the site, Wood Green was the departure point and renamed both Wood Green for Alexandra Park and Wood Green for Alexandra Palace. The branch station survived to 1954 and Wood Green was again the main station for the site leading to the facility being rechristened Alexandra Palace in 1982.

THE GLORIOUS YEARS OF THE GNR – STATIONS

BIBLIOGRAPHY

Allen, C.J. *Titled Trains of Great Britain.* 1983.
Griffiths, Roger and John Hooper. *Great Northern Railway Engine Sheds Volume 1: Southern Area.* 2001.
Griffiths, Roger and John Hooper. *Great Northern Railway Engine Sheds Volume 2: The Lincolnshire Loop, Nottinghamshire & Derbyshire.* 1996.
Griffiths, Roger and John Hooper. *Great Northern Railway Engine Sheds Volume 3: Yorkshire & Lancashire.* 2000.
Groves, N. *Great Northern Locomotive History Volume 1: 1847-1866.* 1986.
Groves, N. *Great Northern Locomotive History Volume 2: 1867-1895 The Stirling Era.* 1991. Second edition.
Groves, N. *Great Northern Locomotive History Volume 3a: 1896-1911 The Ivatt Era.* 1990.
Groves, N. *Great Northern Locomotive History Volume 3b: 1911-1922 The Gresley Era.* 1992.
Harris, Michael. *Gresley's Coaches.* 1973.
Hoole, Ken. *The Illustrated History of East Coast Joint Stock.* 1993.
Jenkinson, David. *British Railway Carriages of the 20th Century Volume 1: The End of an Era, 1901-1922.* 1988.
Leech, K.H., and M.G. Boddy. *The Stirling Singles.* 1965.
Major, Susan. *Female Railway Workers in World War II.* 2018.
Pike, S.N. *Mile by Mile on the LNER.* 1951.
Quick, Michael. *Railway Passenger Stations in Great Britain: A Chronology.* 2009.
Tuffrey, Peter. *Doncaster Plant Works.* 1987.
Tuffrey, Peter. *LNER Workshops.* 2018.
Tuffrey, Peter and Michael Roe. *150 Years of Doncaster Plant Works: A Pictorial History of Britain's Famous Railway Works.* 2003.
Tuffrey, Peter. *The GNR & LNER in Doncaster.* 2013.
Wrottesley, John. *The Great Northern Railway Volume 1: Origins & Development.* 1979.
Wrottesley, John. *The Great Northern Railway Volume 2: Expansion & Competition.* 1979.
Wrottesley, John. *The Great Northern Railway Volume 3: Twentieth Century to Grouping.* 1979.

Also available from Great Northern

Gresley's A3s

Peppercorn's Pacifics

British Railways Standard Pacifics

Gresley's V2s

Gresley's D49s

Gresley's A4s

Gresley's B17s

Thompson's B1s

The Glorious Years of the LNER

John Ryan's Express